MW01171745

LUPUS

GOD'S GRACE IS SUFFICIENT

M. ROSETTE CLEGHORN

J. Kenkade
PUBLISHING
Bryant, Arkansas

J. Kenkade Publishing
5920 Highway 5 N. Ste. 7
Bryant, AR 72022
www.jkenkadepublishing.com
Social Media: @jkenkadepublishing

J. Kenkade Publishing is a registered trademark.
Printed in the United States of America
Hardcover ISBN 978-1-955186-42-1
Paperback ISBN 978-1-955186-44-5

This book recounts actual events in the life of M. Rosette Cleghorn according to the author's recollection and perspective. Some of the identifying details may have been changed to respect the privacy of those involved.

CONTENTS

DEDICATION

To the love of my life, the late Rodney D. Cleghorn, without whom those years would not have been possible: Thank you for being my husband, for loving me and giving me the privilege of being your wife all these years. Thank you for your prayers through long nights, and tough times.

To our sons, Kevin, Raymond, and Damon and their wives, who helped me make it through those tough years. I thank you all very much for all your support, but most of all for your prayers and the time you spent with me during the bad times. You all helped each in your own special way. I thank you for being yourself. And for that, **I love you most!**

To Kyle, Cole, Aleigha, Avorie, Emery, Josie, Ethan, Gabe and all my Great Grand Children now and to come;

To all my grandchildren who have been added since the years described in the following chapters: Dawn, Nate, Haleigh, Cole, Kaitlyn, Jimmy, Johnny, and Jase:

I dedicate to you all a legacy of the love of God, a peace that only God can give and most of all God's Grace which I did not deserve yet He so freely gave that I felt during the painfully hard times described in the following chapters. May you always have the same walk with God in good times and bad. May god's grace be with you always is my prayer! I love you all much more than mere words could ever convey!

-Mom & Grandma Cleghorn

INTRODUCTION

LUPUS, by definition, is an inflammatory disease caused when the immune system attacks its own tissues. It is an auto-immune disease, also known as SLE (Systemic Lupus Erythematosus).

Lupus is a terrible disease. No doubt about that. One that there was not a lot known about when I became ill with it back in 1994. Therefore, I want to start by saying: Yes, I went through some very rough times, but you can judge for yourself. I will try to show you good and bad times and how God was there with me all the way. It is now 2022 and I am still here. No matter how big the problem is, what kind of problem, illness, disease, or anything else it happens to be, we have a God who can handle the situation. He specializes in things thought impossible. I am not telling you that bad things never happen to good people; they sometimes do. I guess that is God's plan. I have no idea about those things. I have had some questions myself, but I do know He is in control, and He knows what is ahead. His plans don't always match, fit, coincide, or even resemble what and when we would like it to. I will not tell you if and when you are diagnosed with Lupus or any other disease, you will have the same outcome as me or anyone you know. You may or may not. Only God knows the end before the beginning. There will always be life and death situations. That is called the circle of life. Also in the bible, Jesus himself said, "These things I have spoken unto you, that in me ye might have peace. In the world ye shall have tribulation: but be of good cheer; I have overcome the world" (John 16:33).

No matter what you face, remember God will be with you all the way. For he hath said, "I will never leave thee, nor forsake thee" (Heb. 13:5b).

We should all, sick or well, live each day as if it were our last. We have no way to know when our time is coming to go home to receive our reward. I pray I have lived each day and will forever treat everyone as I would like to be treated. I don't want this disease to in any way cause any pain and discomfort inside me in such a way that it comes out in anger to others. I know we are all human and tend to let things get to us at times. God understands and I hope those close to us also are a little tolerant with us as well. I know I am not perfect in any way; no doubt I have made many mistakes through this journey. God has been my source of strength and without Him I would not have made it this far.

I will tell you, I believe with all my heart, no matter which way things go, God will be there to walk you all the way to the end of your trial. What God doesn't keep you from, He will keep you through.

And he said unto me, "My grace is sufficient for thee: for my strength is made perfect in weakness" (2 Corinthians 12:9a KJV).

The doctor or doctors are very important in the treatment of this and all diseases. I also believe very strongly in the power of prayer.

As you read this recap of my worst years of Lupus, please keep in mind two most important things:

1. I am much closer to my heavenly Father. It caused me to completely stop. I never had time to slow down long enough to really dig into the word of God like I wanted to for a while. I had a chance to read a lot of books by Christian authors as well as short stories of God taking care of people in miraculous ways. I was reading a lot of uplifting, fulfilling reading along with my bible studies. The more I studied and read God's word, the easier it became to witness to people about Him.

2. My husband and I have always been very close, but, we had much more quality time. Between hospital visits, when I was up to it, we would get up and pack our bags and take off. He would just drive. Usually in the mountains for the scenery to relax. We'd lodge wherever we decided to. Also, he took me to my doctor visits when I became unable to drive myself. We sat in the waiting room holding hands and talking. At the hospital, we would hold hands and he would sing to me. The nurses would often turn on their intercom and listen. I was

usually on the same floor (the 5th). It didn't take the nurses and I long to become friends, more like family.

Please keep in mind, lupus and other autoimmune diseases affect everyone differently. It is very important to consult your primary care physician if you have any abnormal symptoms as soon as possible. The sooner treated, the better you will be. They will run the necessary tests and connect you to the proper specialists needed. There is plenty of literature available for any disease or problems you are diagnosed with. You can also find information on the internet for most. First, however, be sure to be tested and diagnosed before researching anything and getting yourself confused. That is only my opinion.

CHAPTER ONE

MY EARLY YEARS

I can hear her now as we topped the hill from our country home, "Almost home and you can lay her down." Just inside, my brother, two years my elder, laid me on the sofa still too weak to move, my eyes barely open. My younger sister had gone to tell my mom I had passed out. This was not an everyday occurrence. That day I had walked with them to the store up the road a little way, as we had many times before. I felt so bad that day to have put that on my brother, that is, when it was all over. I knew nothing about it when it was happening. I very well remember it. Things like that, you don't forget very easily. It wasn't the passing out that has bothered me, it is the fact that I couldn't get home on my own and had to depend on him to carry me. I am sure he did not complain, but it was how I felt about it. I can't remember our ages; however, I know it was before we were teens. My mom got on the scene, took care of me and all was well once again. Of course, she took me to the doctor the next day. Here came more vitamins.

We had a rough day, but it wasn't long before we were laughing, and they were teasing me about what happened. That's what big brothers do. I couldn't say "I am sorry" enough to my brother.

God's amazing grace was at work in my family all our lives. He has been so gracious to us down through the years we could not count the times and ways. Our dad, Loyd L. Brown passed away at age forty-two, leaving his wife, Maggie Lou and eight children: ages five to seventeen. My mom was the very best manager I have ever met. She could stretch a dollar farther than anyone I have ever heard of or seen. We were raised very well on Social Security and a small garden. There was always plenty of food and enough to share with others. We had company dropping by all time. Everyone who knew us, knew my mom was one of the best cooks and bakers in the county. They also knew she had all us girls and she had plenty of food prepared. She seemed to know when and who to expect extra. Whether aunts, uncles, cousins, ministers, or church members, we had them all. One of her favorite things to instill in us was "If we have any food at all, we have enough to share, no matter what it is." I planned to instill those same values in my family someday. Not only food, but clothing. We always got several new outfits and shoes every year before school. We felt very blessed to have a mom who knew how to manage in a way to furnish new clothes and shoes to start school with. She depended on God to help her supply all our needs. She did her part as far as she could take it, and God would take it from there.

I was always anemic and was always sick. Mom would take me to the doctor, and I knew what was going to take place: vitamins, again. That would pump me full of energy for a few weeks, then, it is gone. The only test he could take is a test for anemia. I did have that; however, it probably wasn't all. Back in those days, that's all they could test for. They had no equipment to use for one thing. That is all they knew to test for. They had probably never heard of anything like Connective Tissue Disease.

Every few months I'd be sick again. My body would be so run down for lack of vitamins and nutrition it couldn't hold up and I would become sick in one way or another, just passing out, collapsing, getting an infection, sore throat, any number of things. My body would hurt so bad, but I can't recall having much fever.

When I grew into adolescent years, my physical problems seemed to settle down a bit. I wasn't sick quite as often. I could help outside more for some reason, and it didn't make me hurt as bad or quite as sick. I had no idea why, but I was so very relieved. I could go to school in peace and do my schoolwork without so much discomfort.

When in junior high school, I was given the opportunity to work at school in a program offered to students with only one parent. We could work various jobs. I worked in the office mainly, but I also worked in the lunchroom as well helping the janitor after school. I enjoyed working with the other students and employees alike. This was during school term and some in the summer. This lasted until I graduated, which really helped with the expenses.

My plans after graduation were to attend University of Central Arkansas in Conway, AR. A friend and I already had our acceptance letters and ready to go. One thing was wrong when time came to leave. I needed to stay home and work so my income could go into the household instead of for tuition and books. No one told me I could not go. I just knew how things were. I didn't mind. I knew God would show me the path he wanted me to take.

"For I know the plans I have for you", declares the Lord, "plans to prosper you and not to harm you, plans to give you hope and a future" (Jeremiah 29:11 NIV).

God had my life all planned out for me right down the line. A life of service for Him I just didn't know it yet.

CHAPTER TWO

God's Plan Begins

Shortly after graduation I heard about a local Abstract Company needing someone. I applied for that job. I went to work full time immediately. This was most interesting work to say the least. The owners of the company were special people, nice and kind. I also did a lot of my work in the land records in the county courthouse. I made a lot of new friends there also.

I decided I could help more if I take another part-time at night and on weekends. I felt like my body could take it right then. I was willing to try anyway. So, I had taken a position at a dairy bar south of town. This would be just a couple nights a week and some on weekends.

One Sunday afternoon, a tall, good-looking young man with black curly hair came to my window. His name was Rodney Cleghorn. We knew each other from my attending Vacation Bible School at his church as kids and in school activities. He ordered several frosted cokes that afternoon. He finally had a chance to ask me to go to church with him that night. Of course, I said yes. That was the beginning of a beautiful life together in June of 1968.

We were married in January of 1969. We knew when we met again and renewed our friendship, there was something special about each other. We spoke about that several times down through our life together. We didn't need to know. God knew. He put us there at that place in time.

By 1974 we had welcomed one wonderful blessing from God, a very handsome little boy, Kevin. Now we were welcoming a double blessing, twin boys, Damon and Raymond. God had given us three boys to love, raise and teach His ways, and His word. We feel most richly blessed. What a wonderful trip it has been. I always got really disturbed when we would go out with the boys and people would make the comment, "double trouble" or some other of many we have heard. We would say "No, you have no idea, twice as nice and more, absolutely wonderful, A special gift of God!"

By that time, Rodney was in college at Biomedical school. We had moved to Little Rock close to the college. When he graduated from college, we moved back to our hometown, Sheridan. He had taken a position with a hospital in a nearby town. He wanted us to move close to family in case I needed help with the boys. At that time, they were still quite young. There again, God always knows what we have need of before we do.

Before we were there long, the boys became ill with an ear infection and a cold. The doctor treated them with antibiotics for the infection and cough syrup for the cough. They seemed to be well. In a couple days their fever returned. This kept happening over and over. Then their fever became very high very quickly. He hospitalized them. Their little bodies were so infected inside. Tests were started to find out why the medications were not working like they were designed to. They were unable to eat by now. I don't know how long I had been awake. I know it had been several days.

On about the fifth day, it was found that there was bacterium in their system that prevented the medication from working. They must kill the bacteria out while treating the infection. They had already begun the treatments. I called Rodney and told him the report. He in turn made calls and had a prayer chain going once more. A night or two after that, their doctor came in about 9:00pm. He said, "I came back for you. There is nothing more I can do for them. The medicine is not working so far." I was so not wanting to hear that. I was so tired. I could not think. I had not left their side since I brought them in over 7 days before, except for a few catnaps. I called Rodney again. He made his calls to let everyone he knew to pray, pray, and pray. He had just left a little before to go pick Kevin up who had taken sick. I told him I would be okay and that I just wanted him to take care of himself. I was really scared. I had to turn my babies over to God. He had to heal them. I prayed as I had never prayed before. I could not lose them.

It wasn't long before my sister came in. She said "Lay down, rest. I came to relieve you." I did just that. I fell asleep in no time. It was about 2:30 when I awakened. At first it scared me that I had fallen asleep at all. Then my sister said, "I am glad you are awake. They are better. They took some milk, and it did not come back up. Their fever is down also." I called the nurse to see if the doctor was still in the hospital. He was and came right in. He checked them over well and then ordered lab test. I knew they would be much better now. God had touched them in a mighty way. I couldn't wait. I had to call Rodney and give him the good news. He and I did some rejoicing and praising God together.

There were so many people praying for them then, and in times such as these, you never know whose prayers reach heaven. That is why you need as many people to pray as possible. However, I was told a few months later, they heard my mother pray that night and ask God to put that illness on her and off the babies, because she could fight it better than they could. She woke up the next morning sick. We thought that was unusual. I have never known my mom to be sick at her stomach. I have heard all my life there is power in a mother's prayer. I am also a firm believer there is power in all earnest prayers.

But I know that even now, whatsoever thou wilt ask of God, God will give it thee (John 11:22)

In just a couple of days, the babies went home. They had some strength to gain and mending to do with no fever, infection, or illness. They just had to focus on enjoying life and being babies. I was enjoying them. God had taken care of that.

In a very short time Rodney found the job he had been praying for. He accepted a position at the VA Hospital in the Little Rock he attended his last college classes at. He was pleased to acquire this position. It did not take him long to move up in this area. He loved his job there. I was pleased because he was happy there. I never cared where he worked if he was happy.

As he moved up in the position, he needed to live closer. He oversaw some winter details that needed his immediate attention when they came up. So, in November of 1979 we moved to Bryant, where we have raised our kids all these years.

My husband was a wonderful vocalist all his life. His music of choice has always been Southern Gospel. Now his boys are following right after him, they are just like him. They make a beautiful quartet. They began singing in church, Rodney by himself, then the boys, then all of them together. After a while, people started asking them to come and sing for their church or function. They didn't set out to form a group, but people kept asking. First thing you know, they were booked up on weekends and at times in between on special occasions. That had been a dream of Rodney's his whole life. He was living a dream come true. The twins were about eight years old and the oldest was around twelve. We prayed about it as a family and felt like God was leading us to ministry in music for at least a while. The guys ended up singing almost all over Arkansas and into several surrounding states for about twelve years.

I had not worked from the time I was expecting our first child until the last ones went to school. I went back to work in 1979 after moving to Bryant. I was very fortunate to find some very well-paid part-time positions, some work at home. I had taught myself to work as full charge bookkeeper, both manual and computerized. I can start the books, set the office up for the company either way, run it, full time, part time, or temporary and train others. I had already held positions with Internal Revenue Service, Veterans Administration, Medical Administration, and several other non-governmental organization jobs. There are two reasons I like working these positions:

1. The pain is always there in some areas, but I can ignore it to some degree. There are times when my body tells me I need to take a rest from working. In that case, I try to do that. Then, I don't take another job at the end of that one for a while and let the pain settle down before I get to that breaking point.

2. Also, that lets me take some time off to know my son's peers. By substituting, I get to know what is going on at school not only with the students, but also with the teachers and those in authority over them. That is very important to my husband and me.

CHAPTER THREE

THE PAIN WORSENS—
I NEED YOU GOD

The pain all over had gotten so bad in my body, feet, and legs that it was almost impossible to bear. It was even difficult to buy groceries for my family. By the time I got home, my body would be inflamed and in severe pain. I had difficulty walking. I had been having difficulty with my feet and legs for quite some time, but now it was in my hands and arms. I had to do something about it.

When we moved here, I decided to make an appointment with the doctor here in town. He was very nice and tried all he could and treated all he possibly could. They were all the right things. They were just not the root of my problem. He treated me for all the problems I had developed in addition to the aches and pains like breathing problems, chronic fatigue, degenerative disc disease, anemia, weakness, etc. This went on for a while with no success.

At one point I injured my back and was down for quite a while. I am sure that was because my joints and muscles were weakened from whatever was wrong with my system. Those sorts of problems went on until sometime in 1993.

At that time, I was working a part-time full-charge bookkeeping position for a company who builds churches. When I got up and walked across the room, I had a difficult time straightening my body up as it was in so much pain. I wanted to cry. I managed to hold it in until I made it home.

My husband was working on a landscape job for my boss. I was doing my best to help him with it in the evenings. That was not doing my limbs any good whatsoever. It was making it totally unbearable. After helping him, I would have to put hot, then cold towels on my arms and hands. Part of the pain in my hands was from typing all morning.

I had just taken part-time position also at another company, an abstract company. By doing this, I was issued another insurance policy which became my primary insurance carrier. When it was time to go back to the doctor, this meant I had to change doctors. I went to Dr. Hollis; he was very thorough, as well as very nice. He took x-rays, blood tests and a full work up. He said he knew I had some problems, but he had rather get the test results before he tells me anything so he can be exact. I told him that would be fine with me. The only thing he could tell me right then was that I have spurs on the vertebrae in my neck. This was causing pressure on the nerves down my arms and shoulders. If it is not better in two to four weeks, he is going to do more testing. That was September 9, 1994.

I returned to his office on October 4, 1994. The pain had progressively gotten worse and had spread through more of my body. It was hitting sporadic and various areas of my body. I never knew where next. **I explained how sick I felt inside and out, and how I had to sometimes crawl up the steps to my office at work**. I would also have to rest during lunch and break to be able to make it through the day. I had to take extra strength Tylenol all day long to be able to stay up and keep moving. I had never hurt this bad before. I hated taking medicine, even Tylenol.

To start with, he sent me to the lab in his office. One was an ANA, also known as Anti-Nuclear Antibodies. The other was a Sed Rate. This measures how high inflammation is in your body.

It wasn't but a few days until Dr. Hollis himself called me with the test results. Both tests were positive. I had no idea what that meant. He explained that it meant I could have any number of connective tissue disease, one of which is Lupus. I needed to be tested further to determine which specific one I have. The next step was to send me to a Rheumatologist. He set up the appointment.

My appointment was on November 1, 1994 and was with the doctor of my insurance company's choice, Dr. Smithson. My husband and I were very displeased. I won't go into the reason why at this time, I will just say, I hated to think I had to go back and get my test results. They were supposed to call me with my next appointment when the test results came back. No call came for over a week, so I called them. They scheduled me right away. The nurse said I should have been called right away. My test for Rheumatoid Arthritis (RA) was quite high and my Lupus was positive. The doctor told me when I saw him, "You tested positive for Lupus, but you do not have it." I asked, "So why would you say that?" His answer "I just know you do not."

On December 6, 1994, my PCP sent me to another rheumatologist, Dr. Abraham. One that was very kind, soft spoken and tenderhearted. He did more blood tests and x-rays of my hands and feet. He said he was sure I had Rheumatoid Arthritis and Connective Tissue Disease. He is not sure which one I had. He gave me a cortisone shot and voltaren medication to try.

On December 19,1994, I returned to his office. We never discussed the x-rays. He gave me a paper copy of the report. I think that was mainly to confirm the presence of RA we had discussed last visit. I didn't know what all those words meant; I did know it all hurt. His official diagnosis to me and on paper was:

Polyarthralgias/arthritis, and most likely SLE (Systemic Lupus Erythematosus) or Connective Tissue Disease, 97% sure it is Lupus.

I was very frightened by that news. I already knew there was something serious going on and that it was possibly Lupus. It just hit home for it to be said to me. That was very hard to take for some reason that day. LUPUS. I wasn't ready for that. I didn't want or need that word used in a sentence referencing a diagnosis for me. It was just a little bit too farfetched for me. I felt myself falling apart. I couldn't wait to leave his office. That had turned out to be a bad day for me! I didn't know what was happening to me. I wasn't usually like this. I am one to stay all together and go on accepting things as they come, one thing at a time. I don't like the unknown and this was clearly the unknown. It all crashed down on me like an avalanche from a snow-capped mountaintop. I had to get a grip on myself.

When I left his office, I went outside across the street to the nearest pay phone. I called the one person on earth that could help me, calm my body down and make me feel better about the whole situation. Yes, my husband, Rodney. He and God were the only ones who could do that for me. Like I said, I didn't have them often, but when I did, I knew who I needed. My husband was the same way. We knew we could always count on each other and God for whatever we had need of.

When I was talking to him, I was standing in the mall, on a pay phone, pouring my heart out, very upset. Now, that was not me at all. When I got through, I did feel much better. I guess I must have needed that. My soul must have needed a good washing.

For the rest of the day, I could think of nothing but, "What is Lupus?" "What am I to expect?" "What does this disease really do to you?" Wow! I know nothing. At that moment I realized I didn't want to know a lot about it. At least not now. Not yet. I decided I wasn't going to read any pamphlet, any internet article, nothing that comes in the mail or anything I came across about Lupus for a long time. I just wanted to take every ache, every pain, one day at a time, one doctor visit at a time, one diagnosis at a time, everything I feel, one at a time. I don't ever want to read what most people feel, or what Lupus symptoms are and then think myself into feeling them. I am going to grasp every moment I can, everything as it comes and make the best of it all; making sure my family has as good a life as possible without any disturbance from Lupus problems. I prayed with my whole heart God will give me grace and favor enough to keep the pain and sickness to myself and not inflict it on anyone else, especially my family. Enough that they will still ask my help, no matter what for things they would have normally asked me for or to do because they know not how I feel. Thank you in advance. These are the kind of prayers I prayed all the way home that day, plus others. Just asking my Heavenly Father for His help and guidance.

CHAPTER FOUR

TIME TO LET GO AND LET GOD

From December 19, 1994, through Christmas, I kept getting weaker. My feet and legs were numb in places. I was having bad headaches and periods of disorientations. So many other things were happening that I didn't understand.

Rodney and I were at the mall one night trying to get some Christmas shopping completed when I began to stagger everywhere. When we arrived home, I told him, "I need to tell you about some things I have been experiencing." He was a little irritated at me for not telling him much sooner about the headaches, disorientation, numbness, etc. I can't say I blame him for that. I just thought it would all pass.

I did my best to get everything completed before the holidays, but I just did not make it. Every time I sat down to rest a minute or to just say something to someone, I was so sick and tired, I would fall asleep for two or three hours. Rodney would not wake me. He said he knew I needed it, or I would never have allowed myself to do that. He knew something was wrong because he could feel me trembling all night long every night all over, enough to shake the whole bed. I told him I deal with that 24/7.

Christmas came and we still had a wonderful time with the family, completed or not. I was too ill to stay up any longer, so I excused myself and went to bed as soon as we were finished with the festivities. No one seemed to mind.

Back to the grind—doctor visits, of course. I had an appointment with my Primary Care Physician (PCP) on 12/27/94. I told him about all the new things I told Rodney. Dr. Hollis said he wasn't surprised, but he was very concerned about all of it. He gave me an anti-inflammatory, and some other medication with the prednisone.

After a few days, my breathing became more and more shallow. I often had this problem. This time, it was making me very sore with chest and upper back pain and feeling swollen in my chest and stomach. I also had difficulty keeping my food down. I didn't know what was going on and exactly what was giving me the problems. Was it my lungs? My heart? Why was it so difficult to breathe?

NEW YEAR'S DAY 1995

I slept almost all day. I couldn't stay up. I kept falling asleep and waking up feeling like someone was choking me. My face felt hot and swollen like I was holding my breath. That kept happening all day and all night.

I got up the next morning on 1/2/95 around 7:30 after my husband left for work. I attempted to fix myself a slice of toast and a glass of tea. This took several attempts of having to lay over on the cabinet to keep from falling. By the time I made it back to bed, my inability to breathe was much worse. I thought I might be having an allergic reaction to the prednisone. I called the hospital. Dr. Hollis just happened to be on call, and he returned my call immediately. He said it was not the medicine and I needed to get to the hospital right away. I called Rodney and told him what the doctor said. He said he was on his way. I told him to call back and I would let the phone ring so the boys would answer and tell them I need help please. There was no way I could get ready and get my clothes together. My husband made it home about the same time the kids had my things and I ready to go.

When I arrived at the hospital, the doctor had taken care of my admission papers. Within a few minutes, they had taken blood, started my IV, I was in my room, had my IV Meds started for the disease and IV antibiotics started.

The next morning when Dr. Hollis came in, we discussed the problems with the numbness, tingling, disorientation, etc. He called in a neurologist.

It is now January 4, 1994, and in comes Dr. Phillips. He was a very personable, likeable doctor. However, he was very straight to the point. That is what I wanted and needed a doctor to be at this point in my life. The first thing he wanted was a Cat Scan of my brain to see if he could tell what was going on.

Again, I knew there was something abnormal happening. I was having too many things I did not understand going on in my life. People I knew I should know were coming in my room to see me and I had no clue who they were. Why do I not know them? Some I think I work with, but I have no recollection of who they are. All these things happening, yet I knew God was going to take care of it.

"Behold, I will bring it health and cure, and I will cure them, and will reveal to them the abundance of peace and truth" (Jeremiah 33:6).

I thought I was afraid on December 21, when I was leaving Dr. Abraham's office with a 97% positive for Lupus. Now I have a 100% positive and so many other things going wrong in my body. My brain is going haywire and some things I haven't told anyone yet, except my boss. Things are happening too fast, and I can't think of things when I am with people, I should tell certain things to. Then I feel bad because I haven't told them. I really can't remember what I have told who.

I am awaiting the results of the CT Scan, I had experienced so many emotions, so many feelings. I felt anxious, but at peace; fearful, yet calm; scared, yet I knew God was in complete control. Our timing might be on different levels, we will meet on the same somewhere down the line. Somehow, I wasn't too worried. That doesn't mean I like going through all these procedures. I don't!

According to Dr. Phillips, my CT scan showed I had a slowing of the brain cells in a lot of different areas. I needed two more tests. I needed a Lumbar Puncture or Spinal Tap. Before I can have that, I must have an MRI to make sure I have no blood clots, tumors, aneurysm, or any other warning signs of a foregoing problem on my brain.

In the first place, I am not fond of either of these procedures. The MRI, I am claustrophobic. The spinal tap, I have heard a lot of bad things about. I guess I will see in just a few hours for myself.

> *Okay God, I must do this. You know, I don't want to. The doctors say they need these tests. If it is what you want me to do, let's do this. I am ready. Whatever is your will. If I am going to have to go through all this God, I won't complain. I just want it to somehow help others also. I am strong enough to take it. This is a horrible disease. Please help others with it to catch it before it gets to this stage. In Jesus name. Amen.*

My night with God was interesting and informative as always. I was lying in my bed looking out to the sky feeling as though God had forsaken me in all this, I knew he really had not, but I couldn't feel him. I was in such a mess all over. My body was a lot worse than I thought it was in my wildest dreams. My condition had progressed so fast. I had taken all the medicine, had followed the doctor's instructions to the letter. I was doing everything in my power to get well. There were people everywhere praying for me. I was just asking God why are all these things being done and I am still getting worse? As I was asking him these things, it was as if he said to me in a still, small heart-to-heart kind of way, "You will be okay." This gave me a calm and peace to face whatever I needed to face tomorrow.

The MRI was very loud and wasn't helping my headache any. The technician was nice, put a washcloth over my face then gave me a bulb to hold to signal her in case I needed her.

It wasn't a tight place or a tight squeeze at all as I was expecting. As I began to pray and meditate on God and His grace, it seemed as though the light particles I had been seeing through the darkness came together. They formed a golden stream that came straight from heaven right into my heart. Then once again I heard that silent heart-to-heart voice, "Here, I am right here. I have been here all along." Right then, my fear of the moment left. I began to sing praises and pray for everyone in my family, church, and people I don't even know. Before I knew it, the MRI was over. Now I was waiting on the results and the dreaded spinal tap that I really dreaded!

Rodney usually left the hospital around 9:00 or earlier. When he was about to walk out, Dr. Phillips walked in with the MRI results. He said it was completely clear of all tumors, aneurysms or anything that would prevent us from doing the Lumbar Puncture/Spinal Tap. "I am ready to do the procedure right now." I wanted to say no. I knew he had already told me it was imperative he do it ASAP. He was ready. His nurse was with him and ready. "Okay, so let's do it." So, Dr. Phillips came in and they began.

First, they scrubbed their hands and arms, then, washed my back with iodine. (They had already gone over all my allergy yes and no's). He found the spot in my back. The nurse had hold of me the entire time. The complete procedure only took a few minutes. I felt nothing but tingling down to my feet. I felt a little like I was going to pass out and was sick at my stomach when it was over from nerves. I did that to myself from being uptight for several days over it all.

They laid me down flat on my back very gently on my bed in my room when they completed the procedure. He said I had to lay very still for 4 hours, and the nurses would be in every 15 minutes to take my blood pressure. The nurse came and brought me a sleeping pill.

Dr. Phillips talked to us, Rodney, and me, for a few minutes. He said sometimes it takes as much as two or three months for some of these tests to come back. Then they may come back as negative for two months the third month positive.

Rodney had been very quiet during all that. He just watched. When all that was over, then we had our time together for a few minutes. I wanted him to go get some rest. He had been here all day long and I would be fine.

I could not go to sleep. I think I was afraid I would move. I didn't need to add to my problems. There was no way I was going to sleep until the four hours was up. I just laid there and sang.

Now it was all over with, CT Scan, MRI, Lumbar Puncture, all of it. Maybe I can relax a little bit and not have to dread anything else except the result of the lumbar Puncture. Now that it is over, I am glad Dr. Phillips did the procedure like he did and got it over with. Maybe I can go home soon. I feel so sick, I need to go home and not move.

Well, one of my Lumbar Puncture tests came back on the 2nd day. It was positive for Vasculitis. This is an inflammation of the blood vessels in your body and brain; it is measured from a count of five up. My count was a 7 Plus. I don't know exactly what the plus means. Zero would have been much better, they said. As my sed rate goes up, this will go up also, same as down. So would the vasculitis.

I finally got to go home on the 9th of January. Of course, I had my dos and don'ts and my load of prescriptions to get filled: antibiotics, steroids, etc.

My do list was as follows: get plenty of rest, don't be up a lot, etc. They don't have to worry about that, I couldn't if I wanted to. I have no strength. I don't think I have ever felt so bad in all my life. I don't feel like moving at all. I want to just lay there, not watch TV, listen to radio, read, look at anything, just do nothing. Didn't care about doing anything that required any movement at all. Please don't make me move, not even one finger or eyeball.

CHAPTER FIVE

God's Grace Abounds

*W*hen I saw Dr. Hollis for my appointment on January 16, my sed rate had increased. Now he had to increase my Prednisone by 10 mg per day to 30 mg per day. During the next few weeks, January 23-30, and on into March 23rd, my sed rate continued to increase each time I went to the doctor. By this time, I was on high doses of prednisone. I think around 80mg per day. That was high, but my sed rate was getting up between the 70's and 80's every time it was checked. It had to come down. That meant the vasculitis was getting worse. Not to mention my body is feeling it.

Dr. Hollis decided to try me on Plaquenil to see if it would help the Lupus get the sed rate down. Here we go; we will see. First, I must get my eyes tested for a baseline eye exam or a field test. Plaquenil can cause Retina damage among other things. There seems to be nothing I can do about any of it at this point, If I don't get this disease under control, it can cause irreparable damage to some vital organs, like brain, kidneys, lungs, etc. The medications can cause some pretty serious side effects also, like anemia which would cause a total lack of immunity. In my case, I have fought that problem all my life. Having a jeopardized immune system already. Now I am on two different medications that will be making that a matter even more difficult than ever.

Dr. Phillips, my neurologist, and my PCP, Dr. Hollis both decided to check me out a bit further. It was things I could take care of from home. Dr. Phillips has ordered a Nerve Conduction Studies to see exactly what a lot of the severe, sharp pain and the tingling, sticking pain is in the legs, arms, hands, and feet. He already told me I had a connective Tissue Disease called Peripheral Polyneuropathy. This would tell him a little more about my case and what all is going on with me.

My next visit with Dr. Phillips wasn't until July. By then, he had studied the lumbar puncture test thoroughly as he said he would do. He said everyone's nerves were covered with connective tissue throughout the body. Unfortunately, mine are all damaged in one way or another by the disease. They are sore, inflamed, infected, or damaged in any number of ways. They are almost all inflamed and sick. That is why the pain jumps around yet, is everywhere all time. This damaged tissue can cause numbness, weakness, severe pain, tingling, etc.

That explained a lot of what I had been experiencing and in essence solved a lot of unanswered questions. That was somewhat of a relief to at least to know what was going on inside.

I have been having a lot of problems with my gastric system for a while now and is progressively getting worse like everything else has. Dr. Hollis thought it might not be a bad idea to check and see if I had a blockage. This procedure was on February 3rd by Dr. Silas, a Gastroenterologist. This showed the swelling and pain was coming from diverticulitis and mucus colitis. I also had a lot of polyps. I did not have a blockage, thank God for that.

One test my Neurologist wants me to have is one to test my brain in thinking and memory ability. I have had a problem thinking clearly with my sed rate being high. The plan is if my body will cooperate and let me, I will be having that on March 15th.

Now that test is behind me. No more, please, not for a while. I just need to rest. I think they tested me on everything possible. It was a long test. I was ready to go to bed. The results: there was a lot of thinking and remembering skills involved. It went well except for short term memory. The Doctor there said that was so bad I could not think properly. I would not be able to work now because I would make too many errors. While my math skills were great, my memory was shot.

I already knew I had a problem with my memory because I could not remember some of the friends that came to see me in the hospital. I knew I should know them, but I just could not remember them and their name. I don't know how many there was. One lady I worked with came to see me. It broke my heart because I tried not let her know I didn't know her. I remembered I loved her dearly, but I could not call her by name.

The doctors all kept telling me to stay down. Don't exert any energy at least until we get the sed rate under control. It will only spread and get worse. It will just do more damage. I couldn't do much to begin with. I had no energy. It was all I could do to move. Not to mention I was in pain all the time. I hated to take pain medicine,

I tried to keep busy. I read a lot of books by Christian Authors like Max Lucado, Charles Stanley, Beth Moore, Guidepost Books, and any number of Christian books by many Christian authors. I also love reading books about Angels. They intrigue me and my curiosity. They are precious beings sent by God.

I received many calls from my church, family, and work friends. It was always nice to hear from them. When I felt like it, I would crochet or sew something,

I also helped with a church project. A friend at church and I sent out cards to those who were sick or shut in or having any kind of difficulty each week. That was a nice job for us both. We got to spend time together working on a project and praying for others who needed help from God.

By March 9, 1995, I had gotten worse upon my return PCP doctors visit. That same thing was happening every doctor visit I went to just about. My doctors, Dr. Hollis and some others had told me the first time I was in the hospital after I was diagnosed with Lupus and having complications with it, I needed to go ahead and file for my Social Security disability. He said he did not see me going back to work any time soon. Not for a while if ever. I decided to discuss that with Dr. Hollis when I went to him that day. I did ask him about this. He said that was my only option at this time. There was no other way for me to have an income. He is going to do everything he could to help me. He said this disease was unpredictable.

That is not at all what I really wanted to do. I discussed it with my husband, we prayed about the whole situation. We felt that was what we needed to do at this time. Soon after that, I called and filed over the phone. They sent me some. Now we wait to receive the paperwork to fill out and take or send back in. When I completed that, we delivered them to the Social Security Administration, Disability Division. Now we wait to receive their decision.

CHAPTER SIX

DOUBLE BLESSING

efore I had to go in the hospital and was still working around town, I found out there was an opening in one of the county offices. I told my daughter-in-law about it. She applied for the job. She was hired. They were staying with us until they could find a house up here. They were moving from another town. My son is already working here. It was a blessing she was hired so quickly.

Not too long after they moved in here, Rose, took a pregnancy test; it was positive. We were going to be grandparents. Our oldest son and his wife are having twins. We have twin sons and now having twin grandchildren. What a great God we serve. How blessed we are.

Now we are receiving more good news. Another blessing is coming to our family. Our third son, Raymond is getting married to a beautiful, sweet, young lady, Missy. A new daughter to welcome into our family. Looking forward to all of them.

MOM'S STROKE

No matter how sick you are or what is going on in your life, the world keeps revolving around you. My mother has always been a big part of my life. We talked several times a week by phone and when I was able, I usually went to check on her every week. If she needed us to, we made more than one trip a week. With the other siblings and I, she was very well taken care of.

Our world, as we knew it all these years, changed on May 1, 1995, with the care of our mother. She had always been an independent lady, living alone since we had all married and left home. However, that changed in just a few minutes. My sister called and said mom had a stroke and was taken to the hospital. She was there five days, paralyzed on her left side and was then sent to rehab. The therapist and doctors there informed us that she could never be left alone again. She would not be safe. Once she got out of the hospital and therapy, we had to all work together to try to accomplish that.

The rehab center gave us the name of the agencies to contact for assistance so we could have that lined up in advance. That was a big help. She wanted to go home. That was our wish too, to keep her stable and in her own environment. We were all willing to try it. Everyone worked, except myself and that was only because I couldn't stay up and go. I was not quite sure how that was going to work out. I was going to try to do my part. God had to give me what I needed. I knew my siblings would understand. I just didn't know if my mother would or not. We all loved her very much and wanted to do what was the best for her and make sure she would get the best of care possible. Time would tell.

She went to my sisters for the first month before going home so we could see how things was going to work out for her in a home setting. She was still adamant to go home. So, we got it all set up to go to her home.

We had all the help we could get, plus we all stayed when we could. Everyone took turns when they were off work, hiring people, etc. We had a young lady, a grown woman with a little girl, live there with her for a while. I stayed as much as possible. I couldn't drive that far, lift her, or push her wheelchair around at that time so I had to come when someone could come and help me. Really none of the girls were able to be lifting mom in and out of her wheelchair. We were not very large, strong women. My youngest sister wasn't hardly one hundred pounds. Mom couldn't even transfer herself. It was getting more and more difficult for everyone.

I would go on weekends when my husband could go and take me so he could help me. By the first of August I was having to cancel my time to stay. I was so sick, legs swollen twice their size, pain so bad, having to take cortisone shots and just couldn't go. My sed rate was in the 90's again.

The following weekend I decided I would try again to go help do my part and stay with mom. I was sicker than ever by the first few hours. I couldn't breathe. My heart was fluttering up in my throat every time I exerted any energy at all.

By the next day, I was even more short of breath. I went to the doctor at my regular appointment, my sed rate was even higher. He said to go back home, get ready and come back into the hospital while he got it set up. At the hospital he found congestion in my chest, quite a bit, bronchitis, pleurisy, swelling in my chest cavity. He also said the Lupus had attacked the Connective Tissues in my lungs. I told him about the fluttering in my heart. He said if it happened again, let him know.

About 2 o'clock that night, the nurse asked me if I had a heart problem. I told her what had happened. She said if it happens again to let her know, I called her later when it woke me up with a jolt. She called Dr. Hollis' assistant. He ordered a halter monitor for 24 hours and called Dr. Wallace, the cardiologist, He came in the next day. He ordered an ultrasound of my heart, said it's okay and that I could go. The cardiologist said if it reoccurs to go to the hospital or to the doctor's office and have an EKG run right then. Well, it happened on Sunday. On September 3rd I got up feeling very ill. My heart was pounding, fluttering and I was having a problem breathing. Rodney took me to the hospital. They gave me oxygen for three or four hours. They also ran an EKG several times. It's worse until it gets better. They sent a copy of them to Dr. Hollis as well as Dr. Wallace. When I arrived at Dr. Hollis Office, Dr. Wallace had sent him a copy of the ultrasound from the hospital. He said the test showed I had inflammation in the lower part of my heart and fluid in the cavity around it or myocarditis and paracardial effusion. In other words, Lupus has attacked my heart now.

Well now, I am even more disgusted with me and this stupid disease, I want to scream, or cry, yell or something. That would do no good whatsoever to help, stop or heal it.

My definition of Lupus is: *It is like a huge cancer inside that is growing and growing and spreading, but you can't see it. You can't detect it. You can't find it until you are inflamed with it. Your body is encapsulated with it before you know it. You are so sick at times you don't want to move, you can't move, can't breathe, can't function and you don't know why. You are swollen either from the disease or the medicine or both. You have rosy cheeks, medicine or butterfly rash, or part of the disease symptoms. Either way people tell you how healthy you look because of them no matter how bad you are or feel. You smile and say, "Thank you".*

Even though all this may have been happening to me and may be happening to all those who have this disease and any other I do know this: Our God made this body that you feel is falling apart a little at a time and it only took Him Six days to create the world and all the nation, and He can restore you and sustain you through it all.

I have never asked God "Why me" But I have often wondered, "Why all this? What are you trying to show me? What do you need me to do? Just Show Me, God."

I just keep trusting God for his healing touch and to go with me through all the valleys. God said He would never leave us.

And lo, I am with you always, even to the end of the age. Amen Matthew 28:20b NKJV

And He said unto me, "My grace is sufficient for you, for My strength is made perfect in weakness."

"Therefore, most gladly I will rather boast in my infirmities, that the power of Christ may rest upon me" (2 Cor.12:9 NKJV).

SOCIAL SECURITY DISABILITY UPDATE:

It took them right at three months to let me know they had denied my claim. I can appeal their decision and they tell me how to go about accomplishing that mission, that meant here we go again through the entire process, only with the Disability determination office. I began praying about this, but for some reason I just could not get excited about it. It could have been for a lot of reasons so I don't think I am going to speculate on why.

CHAPTER SEVEN

WEDDING DAY ALMOST HERE – TEAMWORK

It is almost Wedding Date for Raymond and Missy. That meant it was time for me to get the menu together for the rehearsal dinner and purchase the groceries for it within the next two days. I almost had it all figured out in my head. I didn't know yet who was going with me to purchase everything.

I am really having a hard time having to depend on someone to help me do things. My husband goes with me to do all that sort of thing, but occasionally, some of the kids pitch in and help; especially when it is something out of the ordinary. They would help more, but we don't require much help. The main places we go is to doctor visits.

I had a wonderful day with my oldest son, Kevin today. I see him very little with him helping his wife getting ready for the twins plus his work and school schedules. He came and took me to purchase all the things I needed for the rehearsal dinner.

I mostly gave directions riding in a cart. He did the work. He also carried them in the house for me and put them up. To me that is as hard as going to the store and getting them. It was a very nice day with my son that I would never have gotten accomplished otherwise.

When he finished helping me, Kevin went to take his wife to the doctor for her checkup. He said it was one of the most beautiful twin pregnancies he had seen. They could come any time, or it could be a few weeks. We are excited and patiently waiting.

It is September 27, 1995, two nights before the rehearsal dinner. We are getting a head start on one hors d'oeuvre now so we will have more time tomorrow night.

This was a memorable day for Raymond and Missy for sure. To begin with, it was Missy's birthday. They went and got their Marriage license today. Raymond's "special making memories event" was on the day his wedding party tuxedos were to come in, the owner of the rental store called and informed me they were lost in New York somewhere and they hadn't been able to find them. They had been shipped to the wrong place. Also 30 minutes prior to finding out they were lost; the measurements had been thrown away and in the garbage truck. After frantically searching for the measurements and the Tuxedo's he managed to contact everyone, retrieve new measurements, and save the day. I was very impressed with him. Not only did he work very well with Raymond and all the guys, but he told me on about the third or fourth time he called, "The Lord said He would not put any more on us than we could bear."

I needed to hear that, especially today and tomorrow. God always knows what we have need of. He knows the next few days were going to be hard. I needed to be reminded no matter how difficult it may seem, if I was going to do this rehearsal dinner for my son and his new bride to be, I had to draw from His strength, no matter how He sent it my way. A reminder that He is there. He cares and He will carry our load. HE carried our cross up calvary's hill and laid down His life for us. He is not going to leave us stranded now.

Now to get to work, I had the best help ever tonight. Keela and Rose got to work on the meat, vegetable, and cheese trays. We also had dips and desserts to do. I worked on desserts. We just all worked on whatever was needed. The girls worked very hard and got a lot done quickly. They did an outstanding job. The trays were beautifully done.

Keela and I tried to keep Rose with her feet elevated. Bless her heart, when we finished and came back in the living room, they were so swollen they looked as if they were going to burst. Keela told her they looked like cabbage patch dolls feet. I could not have made it without these two girls. Thank you so very much.

The day of the rehearsal was here. The only thing left to do was to put last minute touches on things, get them covered ready for traveling and go. I have also got to fill the baskets for the Bride and Groom and their guest tables. Kevin came and helped me get everything to the church early then Rodney came when he got off from work. By the time we got there, Damon, Keela and Rose were there. Rodney wasn't far behind. Everyone got the tables all set up and everything set out, by that time, everyone was there, ate, went to rehearsal. We then cleaned the dining hall. Our part was complete. I never would have made it without all my helpers: Rodney, Damon, Keela, Rose, and Kevin. They were my life savers and did most of the work for me. They were a hard-working crew the last few days. Everything went perfect, thanks to all of them. Thank you all so very much.

I went in the church and rested and enjoyed watching the rehearsal. Rodney helped Missy's family for a few minutes set up for the wedding reception.

Raymond and Missy were both very nervous. Raymond was doing his best not to show it. Of course, with our bunch there was always going to be a lot of laughing, joking, and playing around while any kind of get-together is going on, but the job always gets completed on time. That helped calm everyone a little bit. The Pastor was finally able to get them through the rehearsal and finished so everyone could call it a night.

This was it for the wedding plans except for the wedding itself. We are looking forward to that tomorrow. That is except for one big problem, my health. I am really going through a lot the last few weeks. I have had to increase my meds again and have gained a lot more weight again. Not to mention the severity of the pain and other problems the inflammation brings. I am praying my family hasn't picked up on it being up and around them so much. I made it through the last few days without too much difficulty. God's grace was sufficient for then and I am sure it will be for tomorrow.

And He said to me "My grace is sufficient for you, for my strength is make perfect in weakness" (II Corinthians 12:9).

Today is the day, I had to get going, lots to do. *Okay God, this is your day to really shine in my life. I need your strength today. Mine is gone. My legs are too weak to take me where I must go. I am depending on you today. Thank you for all you are going to do today.* This day, I was so weak, I would have stayed right where I was. Not that I didn't want to go, but I knew how difficult it was going to be without God. My legs felt like spaghetti. But here we go. Rodney and I went by the church for a few minutes. Then he took me to a friend's beauty shop. She was going to do my hair, makeup and try to tone down the redness and the swelling in my face. I told him when I got out of the car, I didn't know if I could make it or not. He said, "Don't worry about it, honey, I will catch you if I am where I can. Hold on to my arm. If you start to fall, I will at least break your fall and I will carry you in there." *God where is your strength? Please help me to stay upright and not get hurt or cause Rodney any embarrassment or myself either. Just let me get inside and I will be resting for a while before going on to the church. Please God.* I started praying to myself as I was trying to make it to the door. Just as I was about to make it to the door my legs gave way with me and down I went, right outside on the sidewalk. Rodney helped me on into the shop. I wasn't hurt much. Neither was my dress. Rodney had done what he said he would do and broken my fall, my legs gave away with me and I just went down. We proceeded with the rest of our day. I was just weak the rest of the day.

We returned to the church around 10:00, took care of our part of the preliminaries we needed to. Checked on the bride and groom. They were very beautiful and handsome. The wedding started precisely at 11:00. It was just beautiful. Her gown, his tuxedo, the song he sang to her, and the pastors and their speech were all just beautiful. It all went off great.

Just a note: I hope you didn't mind going down that road with me. I wanted to show you sometimes you just must take care of life's wonderful little tasks we have the privilege of doing that we love to do for our loved ones. We might feel more like doing them at another given time. However, that isn't possible. **This is the time and place that has been allotted for this project to be fulfilled by you and for you to perform. These kinds of things are some you would never want to give up the chance to do for those you love no matter what your body goes through during it**. They mean a lot to a lot of people. They should.

The scripture, II Corinthians 12:9, I put a little above in this document and the title of this book, is what carries me through a lot of difficulties. It carries me through every day, especially extra hard days like the last few. Days like these are the ones I must keep praying my ever-present heart prayer since the onset of this disease:

Lord, help me keep my heart, brain, and words in check that I will not let this disease influence or change anything in my family's life at all. They will have a happy, wonderful life. I knew my husband knew more than I wanted him to know because he said he feels my body trembling at night. He says it felt like being in bed with a vibrator. I just laughed and told him he ought to feel pretty good every morning after being massaged all night. He just told me I am crazy. Haha.

However, I would not change one single thing about the last few days for anything at all. I loved every minute of it. Every moment we spent together we were making another moment of memories. Wow, what nice memories they were. We laughed, talked, shared, and worked together and did a lot for Raymond and Missy. Thank you everyone.

Kevin received a piece of very important mail on September 29, 1995. He passed his tests and received his Certificate or License and is a Registered Emergency Medical Technician. Now he is ready to begin paramedic school.

CHAPTER EIGHT

BUNDLES OF JOY ARRIVE

*N*ow it was time to switch gears and get some rest. I had to get this sed rate down and get this swelling down before the babies are born. They are due in less than three weeks but could come any time. In the next few days, that's what I did. I did nothing except rest. I really wasn't feeling like it at all. I was supposed to go see my PCP on October the second. I just wasn't up to going by myself and I didn't tell anyone. I just called and told them I would have to come get my blood tested tomorrow. I did that and all that extra medicine I have been taking has evidently been doing something after all. My sed rate came down two points. At least it did not go up again. He said leave everything as is even the bed rest. I was very concerned about going out today with just a cane. I was going to have to talk to some doctor about it. I was very uneasy. I was ready to collapse. And that I did on the sofa just inside the door. There I stayed until Rodney got home.

I had a very nice surprise when I got home from the doctor's office today. I received a call from a very special lady from the Abstract company I worked for when I became ill. She said the girls from the office wanted me to come to the office tomorrow at 10:00. They had a surprise for me. I was excited and sad too. I missed them so much. They were the best ladies in the world to work with. I was anxious to see them.

I had a rough night. I couldn't breathe, and when I tried to, electrical shocking pain would shoot all over my body. I was hurting in my chest, my legs, especially my left one.

This is going to be a wonderful day, it must be. I need this day out with friends. I am not going to let Lupus beat me out of this day out for a change. So, I was finally able to get my medicine and eat a little bit. After a while I was feeling some better. Not great, but God gave me enough strength enough to try it. Here we go, my walker and me.

When I got to the abstract company, a wonderful friend and boss and the girls had cake and ice cream for me. The big surprise was a very large box filled with all sorts of "goodies for grandma". There was anything I will need at my house for my grandbabies. There were thermometers, handwipes, receiving blankets, medicine droppers, measurers, nipples, spoons, under shirts, and lots more. Like I said, they are the greatest. We visited a while. I told them how the disease had damaged the inside of my body, my organs, etc. and how they were treating me, why the swelling and weight gain, there is no cure, but can go into remission. I hugged everyone and thanked them as they went back to work. Now I needed to go upstairs and clean my desk out. That was a problem to climb the stairs. Two of the girls went with me to help me. As I tried to climb, I had to go very slow. They were patient with me. I started laughing at myself, so they were laughing with me. When I finished, they helped me take all my things to the car. By then we were all crying. It proved to be a very emotional day for all of us.

I had a wonderful day with my friends at the abstract company. We laughed, cried, opened presents for the grandbabies, and ate. Thank you again for a pleasant day and nice gifts for my grandbabies. They were very well used.

It is almost time for our grandbabies to be born. I have been busy trying to get everything ready to welcome them home either at our house or at their house when they come home from the hospital. I think they are going home. I am working on everything I still must wash a little at a time between resting times. I am doing my best until then, to get plenty of rest. So far I have gotten quite a bit every day. I have been feeling a little stronger the last couple of weeks. The medicine the doctor gave me just before the wedding has helped me some. I hope it will continue to keep me stronger. Now I just wish it would do something better about the pain. It is a very little better.

Late on the night, Rose was in a tremendous amount of pain, so the ambulance was on their way to pick her up, and Kevin worked for the Ambulance service.

I don't know when everyone arrived. It was Rodney, Rosé's mom, Raymond, Missy, Damon, Keela and me. I don't know if there were any others. She was in labor most all night. Everyone got there long before the doctor said he was ready for her to start pushing.

They had it arranged with the doctor where her mother and I could be in the room with them when the babies were born. That was the most special thing anyone had ever done for me in my entire life. It was a very precious thing to me.

Somewhere around 11:00-11:30, she was told to start pushing. That meant we had to put on our blue paper uniform head to toe while the doctors and nurses helped each other get scrubbed and suited up themselves. They also had to get the room ready for two little ones, two incubators ready, two of everything for the babies. Also, all the instruments for Rose, plus break the bed down for the delivery. Quite an experience to watch it all. It had been about 20 plus years since the birth of our twins.

At 1:00 p.m., on 10/19/95, our first grandson finally made his appearance in this world. At 1:23, our second grandson made his appearance. Their names were Kyle and Cole. Perfectly healthy. Born one day past their due date. God was so gracious to us in their birth and her pregnancy. She had a perfect pregnancy and a beautiful delivery. It could not have been more beautiful. They both weighed over five pounds, nothing wrong with either one of them. Of course, we grandmas got to hold them right away as soon as the nurses finished with them. Grandpa got to hold them when he got to come in. Wow, what a time we have had this afternoon!

There were several times I stopped and thanked God for all the blessings He had sent our way that day. It probably sounded a lot like this prayer to God below. This is the feelings that my notes in my journal stirred up in me about the happenings of that day.

God you are so good to us. Your blessings are so amazing. I have asked you, God so many times, to keep my family safe, strong, and healthy. Always put them first! Put me on the back burner, I am a fighter. I am strong. I can take it. Give them favor. Thank you for answering my prayers now and in the future. Remember this for all those coming on later, please. In Jesus name. Amen.

We went home to rest for a while. Rodney and I had been up for more than 12 hours. We were both worn out. We had prayed for each other before we went to the hospital the night before. He had been tired, but not quite as sleepy as I thought he would be. He prayed for my breathing and my pain. I did okay. I had to use my inhaler and pain medication some, but it could have been worse.

With this disease everyone seems to be fighting a never-ending battle no matter what kind of joys or hard times you are experiencing in life. However, God is always there fighting them with you, and He will sustain you, just go into everything you face knowing He goes before you. "Cast your burdens on the Lord and He shall sustain you" (Psalms 55:22a NKJV).

And the Lord, He is the one who goes before you. He will be with you. He will not leave you nor forsake you; Do not fear nor be dismayed" (Deuteronomy 31:8 NKJV).

Rodney and I had to be back at the hospital around 6:30. or 7:00 to have a very special family prayer service with all of us for the first time together. This was our dedication service for the twins. Damon sang "Another Child to Hold". Everyone was crying. Kevin prayed a beautiful prayer for God's guidance and protection on the babies especially. He asked God to increase the closeness of the family among other things. It was a day inspired by God.

My plans right now are to go home, take a hot shower, get ready for bed, go to bed, and get a good night's sleep without setting an alarm.

SOCIAL SECURITY DISABILITY UPDATE:

On September 23, 1995, I was home alone when the mail ran. In it that day just happened to be a letter from Social Security Division, Department of Human Services. As I opened it, the word "Denied" was the significant word I saw. When I talked to Rodney at work a few minutes and then at home that evening, we decided to go ahead and hire a lawyer. They charge on a contingency fee. That is, you do not pay anything if they do not get any money for you. I am disappointed that it will be another while again; more waiting.

On the following week, Sept 25, 1995, I consulted a lawyer. Our appointment was October 5,1995. The receptions had put me in touch with a lawyer familiar with Lupus and what kind of damage and illness it can and does to the people it attacks. He also wanted to know how I felt about it. This gentleman was a very kind, soft spoken person. He was pleasant to talk with. My appointment is April 10, 1996 at 10:30.

CHAPTER NINE

TWIN'S FIRST HOLIDAYS

I was being very careful to take all my medicine just as directed, getting plenty of rest. As a matter of fact, lot of plenty of very relaxing rest. I read a lot, and I did do some things to get ready for Christmas. Not as much as I usually did. I just wasn't feeling well at all for several days. I didn't know what was going on, but I was not well. I thought I might have a little urinary tract infection at times. I just figured I would just drink some cranberry juice and it would be okay right away.

We had a wonderful Christmas holiday with our new grand-babies and our new daughter, with all the family and friends. We laughed, talked, ate, then we moved in the living room for Rodney to read the bible story of the birth of Jesus. This year Kevin did the honors. He read the passage from the second chapter of Luke. This has always been our tradition. Jesus first, then we exchanged gifts.

In a few hours everyone started going home after we finished cleaning the table and kitchen up. Rodney and I were both tired, so we went on to bed quickly, I sooner than he. I was still a little tired the next day but feeling better. I changed my appointment with my PCP to the 28th so I could take care of some business I needed to take care of. I thought I was okay now. I was just as tired as usual.

The day went okay. That night at 2:00 in the morning, I woke up with a rigger and in such severe pain all over, especially my legs and back. Rodney got me two pain pills and two Tylenol. My body finally settled down and I went back to sleep. I was fine the rest of the night and seemed to be feeling pretty good the next day. I had some pain, but not too severe, no more than some of my normal pain. I was feeling quite a bit more fatigued and weaker than normal, but I did that sometimes. I really felt something was just not quite right, but I just could not figure it out. My thoughts were my sed rate was up and maybe I had another bladder infection. I knew the pleurisy had been bothering me a lot. All of it together was just too much on me and getting me down.

At around 11:00 that night I did the same thing again. I became very ill with a hard rigger. I was weaker in my left side. I had made an appointment with Dr. Hollis for 10:00 the next morning. When that time came, I almost didn't get myself dressed, much less drive myself to the doctor. I called a very sweet lady across the street and asked her to take me. She graciously said "Yes, I would be happy to."

Things did not turn out like I had hoped it would. He said I had bacteria in my kidneys, bladder and my urinary tract. Then he said wait and let me check your blood. He came back and said it is already in your blood also. He said your next move is to go to the hospital. You have got to have IV antibiotics.

The next at the hospital, the doctor told me the test showed the bacteria was confirmed to be a very serious one, not yet named. He was going to start my IV at a very fast pace to flush me out and up my IV to a higher dosage to try to get it killed out fast. He would be checking the labs to see how well they are coming down to see when I can go home.

I came in on December 28th, it is now January 3rd, I am still in the hospital. No indication I will go home today. Maybe tomorrow. That would be nice. That was Rodney's and my Anniversary, so that would be a very nice day for me to come home. Morning came and Dr. Hollis made his rounds. The first thing he said was that the bacteria in my system and in my blood was E-COLI. It had been very deadly. It was better then. If it was a little better the next day, I may can get the IV out. I am thinking I might can finish my antibiotics at home.

January 5,1996, home at last! Yes, home with antibiotics and more orders to come back January 10.

January 10, 1996, it is now time for my visit. The bacteria in my system and my sed rate is a whopping 92. I am to come back when I finish the antibiotics. That is if I am not rushed back to the hospital by then. So many things can go wrong with all this stuff in my body and the sed rate so high that makes the danger that much worse. The doctors had already told me of the dangers of my sed rate being so high, like stroke, seizures, convulsions or worse as they said. Also, vasculitis and high sed rate does not mix with all these bacteria. I just know this old body is sure tired dealing with all these problems at the same time.

I sure miss a lot by being sick. I miss my family's singing. Sometimes I go with them and end up laying down in the car most of the time, at least Rodney is not worried about me at home or feeling like he had to stay with me.

I am missing seeing the twins. The doctors tell me I am not contagious, but I will not get around them while I have something like E-Coli. I couldn't stand it if I gave them something like that and they got sick, or anyone else either. I just will not take that chance.

I had to return to the doctor on the 17th of February, to have my blood checked. That nasty old bacteria were still plaguing my body. He had put me on high doses of oral and IV antibiotics. It had not killed it out only helped it. The doctor decided to try giving me sulfa drugs for two weeks and come back and see if they had helped. I could tell they were making me sick at my stomach. I hoped it was worth it. I went back to the doctor after two weeks, by then I was feeling better, not shaking so bad and not quite as weak. Rodney had taken me that day. We had the twins with us too, so we could take them by the Abstract Company to see the ladies. They were so excited. We laughed, cried, and played with babies. We all enjoyed every minute.

Rodney took us back home so he could go to his job on his second job. I am sure hoping he can quit that job soon. I am hoping and praying my Social Security comes through soon.

So once again, the doctors said, I would not be going back to work for a long time and I need to file for my disability, which is a work in progress. I don't mind that as bad as it breaks my heart that my husband thinks he must work two jobs until I get my disability started. I keep trying to get him to quit his part-time job, but he won't. I keep praying and expecting God to allow me to be able to at least wake up and get out of bed and walk from room to room in my own home without help or aid of any sort and feel comfortable to do something for myself by myself. I want to be able to help my family again, and I will soon. I am not so brave when I go out, my wheelchair, walker, or just a cane, whatever I feel my body needs that day. I just do not want to fall and break a leg or worse. I take every precaution I possibly can. Until then I am standing on this scripture:

"Be careful for nothing, but in everything by prayer and supplication with thanksgiving, let your request be made known unto God, and the peace of God, which passeth all understanding, shall keep your hearts and minds through Christ Jesus" (Phil: 4:6&7 KJV).

CHAPTER TEN

God Sends a Big Surprise

*E*ven though so many things were happening around us, a silver lining for those gloomy clouds was bound to show up some time.

I was feeling some better now and things were settling down a bit. Raymond and Missy surprised us with a visit tonight. We were so pleased to see them. We were even more excited to hear their special surprise they had to tell us. They are going to have us another grandchild. Rodney and I were so excited and surprised. She had taken a test and it was definitely positive. We don't have a preference of the gender of the baby. We will be pleased no matter which one. They have made an appointment with the doctor to get started with her prenatal care. This was wonderful news. Now we are expecting our third wonderful grandchild. I just wanted to concentrate on that new baby we are expecting. If it is a girl, I can make her dresses, crochet her sweaters, and blankets any color they want. But I did for the boys too. Just changed the patterns. I am so looking forward to it. The first girl in the family.

Back to the old grind, doctors' visits as usual. Dr. Hollis is now sending me to an internal medicine specialist. He said my sed rate had just been too high too long. I had to get it down and keep it down. It had been out of control for over a year and Dr. Hollis wants to get a second opinion. He wants me to get a second opinion. I went and did as my doctor asked. He was a very nice doctor. I didn't like his opinion very much, however it did match several other doctor's opinions. He said, I have seen very few Lupus patients or any others with a sed rate of 90 and above and yours has not been in the 20's but once at 28 but once a year ago. We don't like to see them in the 20's at all. You could go one of two ways. One, you could rock on like this and go in remission, or two, the Lupus could start attacking your vital organs. I see it is already doing that with the myocarditis, pericarditis, your lungs and all the kidney problems. Although your kidneys don't seem to be significantly damaged, but I know God can heal me. I don't want to live like this for a long time. I can't imagine for years to come. It is a good thing we have a God to turn to for strength and courage.

No matter how bad I feel, life goes on. I do my best to struggle through it all. The good and the bad. In the last few days, several things have taken place. One thing I am glad about is my husband quit his second job. I hope maybe, he will get some rest now and not look so tired.

Another visit to Dr. Hollis meant another increase in my prednisone. My sed rate was increasing and so were my symptoms of my vital organs, heart, lungs, and my ability to think and my coordination. I hate taking that medicine and he doesn't like having to give it to me. However, there isn't anything better. Another chance for God to work on my behalf. I have just got to rest a little more and take a little better care of myself. I know when I feel like I need to get a task accomplished, i.e., Laundry, perhaps a meal prepared for my family, I get and do my best at trying to do just that. Sometimes I might have to lay down a few times before I get the job completed or even turn it over to someone else to finish. I know without a doubt, at times, I had no business trying to start it in the first place. I had no energy to start with at all. There have been times when I didn't feel like I had any energy and I tried doing things anyway, took a chance, without my cane, walker or wheelchair and my legs just crumpled on me, in the house, down the steps, coming in the door, wherever they decided. Thank God, I have never gotten injured other than rakes and scrapes, skins, and bruises. I think I get so tired I am not very stable on my feet. I am so weak; my legs won't hold me up. I guess God takes care of me. I am too weak to try to go anywhere with my grandsons anymore. I don't drive anyway. I took myself off driving until I get to feeling better and not so disoriented at times. It doesn't bother me at all to tell my son and daughter-in-law "I would be glad to help you with them, but I am not feeling up to keeping them by myself today." They had rather me say that than to keep them and something happen that shouldn't. They know how much I love them.

Time has a way of marching right on by. I managed to prepare dinner for my son and his wife and another couple today in spite of all the pain and trembling.

That is something I do not understand about Lupus. The tremors. It feels like a vibrator inside me all time. If I say it hurts so bad it is almost intolerable until I get settled down and relaxed. Sometimes that takes a while. If I keep going, the pain gets so bad, I just collapse from the pain and cannot help myself. I just lose control of the ability to stand. I had to learn to take very frequent breaks.

It was that time for that Sunday, time for medicine and relaxing. My energy was totally gone: what little I had in the first place. That is a big problem with that disease, it depletes your immune system, so you have no energy. That is the reason for taking all the vitamins all my life. Lupus destroyed them as fast as I took them. My body had a way of telling me when something was going wrong, and I need to pay attention to it. *Rodney used to tell me and/or ask me "God said He would not put any more on us than we could bare, but don't you wish He didn't have such a high opinion of you?"* The answer to that is "Yes, I do, and it may get to me physically, but not going to get me down emotionally or spiritually. You see, God and me, we've got this. All the way whatever comes up. I am truly blessed with the family God gave me. They are all Christians and attend church regularly. I thank God they are and have been all these years.

My body is talking loud and clear to me again. It is telling me I need to give it help fast. I can't breathe a lot of the time lately.

My heart is giving me a lot of trouble again. Also, I am experiencing longer and more frequent periods of disorientation. I am trying to deal with too many issues right now. Each one just as important as the other.

There are some that are very important to me that I can't seem to accomplish without getting very ill. That breaks my heart. That is helping take care of my mom. My family needs me to take my turns, but every time I do, I end up in the hospital. It takes all the energy I must do small things at my home, much less try to do that for an hour. Helping my mom or try to help with my mom to transfer. So far, every time I have gone for just one night and day, within one or two days I was back in the hospital very ill. I get too exhausted. I have overworked my muscles, they became inflamed, sed rate elevated, just many problems start happening. It causes all kinds of problems to get that fatigued and low. Breaks my system down. I just start praying when I leave to go help and do the best I can. Rodney always helps me, but some things he cannot do for her.

My son and daughter-in-law let me help with the babies some time. That is more for my benefit than theirs, like I mentioned before so I will relax with them. It is my therapy.

I don't know what I would do without my husband helping me with the housework. He helps me with all the vacuuming, sweeping, some laundry, etc. I try to do most of the cooking. I don't do that on days when I am having trouble with thinking straight or not walking steady. I help as much and as I can.

I decided I wanted to try to prepare a meal for Sunday dinner and invite our kids, and some friends. There were adults as well as a few teens. As I got through with the meal, I felt very tired. I went in the living room to rest. I sat there for a few minutes. I began to feel my breathing beginning to become more and more shallow until I began gasping. I had no air hardly at all. I was smothering. Someone called the ambulance. They were there in just a few minutes. The paramedics administered an updraft to make me start breathing and open my airways. I don't know what caused that to happen, I just know it was very scary. I had an appointment with the doctor the next day, my sed rate had dropped by four points. It was still quite high at 58. Not as high as it could have been by what had happened the day before. The doctor said he was not going to get excited over 4 points. At least we are not moving up. At 58 it is high, but not in the 90's. The ladies in the lab of this clinic call me the queen of sed rate, because mine is always the highest. I told them there was a whole lot of things I had rather be queen of than a sed rate. I am not a prejudice person at all. Who me? Queen? Me? Queen of anything, even sed rate? You have got to be kidding. Haha.

Dr. Hollis said the episode yesterday was caused by a combination of pleurisy, bronchitis and with Lupus on top of that. He said we must get that inflammation down before the vasculitis gets bad again and my brain swells again. Several things could happen. I don't want any of those to happen. Neither do I want to keep increasing my medication. Just that in itself causes fluid weight gain and that can cause you to smother. I must keep hanging on to God's word. I need it to keep me going. Sometimes it gets a little hard with something popping up every day. Never a dull moment around me. You never know what the next one will bring. I try to keep a scripture ready to bring to my memory and on my heart that can help me in any situation. One of the scriptures I would repeat and read were and still are:

"I can do all things through Christ who strengtheneth me" (Phil. 4:13 KJV).

A FEW DAYS LATER:

When you are a parent, you find a hidden strength to be there for your kid when you are called no matter what is going on in your life. Even though I was going through all that, when our daughter-in-law called and told us Kevin had passed out at church while playing the piano up front. My husband and I went down to the church right away. The paramedics said he had an abnormal EKG and high blood pressure. They took him to the hospital. They kept him overnight and ordered more outpatient tests. A few weeks the same thing happened again. He was taken back to the hospital. This time, they found that due to a wreck he sustained a few weeks prior coming home from work one afternoon, a young lady ran into the side of his car, his chest muscles were bruised and inflamed. It wasn't his heart at all. Thank God. God was definitely there for us on that one. It could have been a lot worse. He is going to be fine.

CHAPTER ELEVEN

GOD, MORE CHANCES TO WORK

I had been doing my best to lean on God for His guidance in dealing with this Renal problem. I was doing everything I have been told to do and taking care of myself as much and as well as possible. The UTI's (Urinary Tract Infections) kept returning. I am now being referred to a Urologist, Kidney Specialist. It is so dangerous because with me it doesn't stop with just a UTI, it goes straight into my blood with E-COLI. This can get very dangerous levels, very fast, as it did with me a few months ago. He ran some test to determine why this is reoccurring so frequently. One of the tests was an IVP (Intravenous Pyelogram). A type of x-ray that provides images of the urinary tract. The urinary tract is made up of kidneys, two organs located below the rib cage. They filter the blood, remove waste, and make urine. This test is when they inject dye in your veins. It goes through the renal system. While it passes through there, the technician takes pictures of that area. I did not want to have that test for several reasons. One of the main reasons was that my poor old veins have just about had all they can take and so have the hospital staff dealing with them. They are probably tired of dealing with me, I have been here so much. They have all been just great to my family and me. I did have within a day or so the results of the IVP: There was no way to see if there was nerve damage to the Kidney. The muscles around the kidneys and bladder have broken down and the lining or inside wall of my bladder (connective tissue) is gone. This is letting the bacteria stick to it and build up. Therefore, the antibiotics are not working. The bacteria is growing as fast as the antibiotic is killing it out.

As you know by now, Lupus is a connective tissue disease which destroys or attacks the connective tissue within your body wherever it desires to attack. The bladder wall has three principal tissue layers or coats: (some say four):

1. Mucosa Submucosa-Areolar Connective

Tissue interlaced with the Muscoat.

2. Muscular layer

3. Serosa

The above information is taken from The Internet, Google, NIH National Cancer Institute Seer Training Module. Layers of The Bladder Wall, so that is what has happened to my bladder. Just as it did to my blood vessels. It attacks the connective tissue on my blood vessels. I was finding out your body had connective tissue everywhere. I had no idea it was all in your body like it is.

Now I must face dealing with my insurance company. My body is shutting down again. It never got up very far at all. I can feel everything, all my strength, my ability to function, stamina, etc. It is all gradually draining out of me, and I can do nothing about it. I am getting sicker by the day, hour, minute.

It is now May 20, 1996. I feel as though God and I have been fighting this battle for years already when it will be only two years this coming May. Wow, it seems like it has been at least ten.

By the following Friday I was very ill. I was so weak I could hardly walk. I went to the doctor with a lot of help from my husband. I needed IV steroids, Solumedrol and to be in the hospital then. That is the best or only thing that will get my sed rate down and the inflammation under control when it is so high. I am not sure what the count was that day, I am not sure I wanted to know. He tried to get an approval from my insurance company, and they said "no". That was the first time they had ever refused to approve anything I needed. There must be an error in the system somewhere. With my insurance company, that doesn't happen ever when a doctor's office calls with a request for something like that. I must have that medicine now. I could not wait for it. My inflammation would only get higher and higher. So Dr. Hollis did the only other thing he could do. He ordered it to be administered at home. He ordered a company, The IV Company, that does that sort of thing in this area to come out to my house and get my IV started as soon as possible.

They got there at 11:00p.m. that night. This was on Friday night. My vein blew the first time. They had a very hard time getting it. They finally got it going. Then on Saturday during the night the vein blew. Blood got on my pillow, bed sheets, pillowcases, a little on my husband, and several other places. It was a mess. Sunday morning the nurse came back out to repair the problem.

This time the RN decided to insert a PICC Line in my arm instead of the IV. A PICC Line is a Peripherally inserted central catheter line, a thin, soft long tube that is inserted into a vein in the arm, leg, or neck. The tip of the catheter is positioned in a large vein that carries blood into the heart. The PICC line is used for long term intravenous IV Antibiotics, Nutrition, or medications, and for blood draws. The PICC Line was put in the bend of my right arm in the vein, up my arm, and across my chest to my heart area. He and our son who is a paramedic tried several times. It was quite an ordeal for them. Everyone does not have that kind of problem. It usually very simple to do all these things. I have small veins and at that time, they had been very overused was the problem. I was bleeding like I was because I was on blood thinners. Another reason was the average or usual dosage of Solumedrol is 60mg. Three times a day, however my sed rate was so high that I had to have higher doses of 125mg three times a day.

All of this was taken care of with me stretched across my bed with everything sanitized. I got no contamination, no infection. No problem at all. The RN was very sanitary and safe with everything. I took all the medication I was supposed to take. I was ready to get all of this out of my body. It turned out to be "no big deal". He knew exactly what he was doing.

It wasn't as bad of an experience as I thought it would be at all. The RN was very gentle with the procedures, and as I said, he knew what he was doing. He made it as pleasant as possible. Not bad at all, even stretched across my bed at home. Sometimes you just do whatever is necessary.

This was just another chance to witness for God. A new nurse, a new company, not a hospital setting, God was still there administering His grace and love. *That is what He did when I was in the hospital, gave me numerous chances to witness to those who needed him in so many different ways.*

UPDATE ON SOCIAL SECURITY DISABILITY

April 10, 1996

The meeting went very well with my Lawyer, Mr. Harris. He was one of the lawyers from a prominent law firm in this area, a very nice, soft-spoken gentleman. He set up another meeting to go before the judge. This was to be on May 1, 1996 at 10:30. I was surprised it wasn't a longer wait than just under a month.

May 1, 1996

The hearing took place in the judge's Chambers at the Courthouse. We sat around a large table. My lawyer asked me questions, my husband, and my friend. They made their comments. It was over. It was difficult to hear my husband tell how our lives had changed since the onset of this disease. Although I knew it was true, I hurt for him. They told us it may be three months to a year before we hear anything. I told Rodney I felt good about this one. It wasn't going to be that long.

May 29, 1996

Rodney and I were still sitting in the car returning from town stopping by our mailbox and there it was. A letter from Social Security Administration. I looked a little closer. In the window, I could see "Notice of Decision". It had only been four weeks since we had gone before the judge. A decision already. This could be either way. We were believing good. I was still a little apprehensive in opening the letter all the way. "Ok honey, Here goes" I paused, "Fully Favorable", I said to him crying. He said, "What are you crying about?" "I was just thanking God for his answers to our prayers, His love, His grace, His mercy, and everything He does for us and it always being right on time. I told Him "Thank You, Jesus for your faithfulness in all things."

They said it would take sixty to ninety days to get the check cut. I am believing for it to come within 20 days. I told Rodney that will be before the eighteenth of June. Thank you, Lord, for the answer to our prayers in advance.

June 14, 1996

Once again God came through for us. We checked our mail frequently from then on, looking for an answer to our prayers. *On June 14, 1996, there it was four days before the 20 days were up. God is so awesome, and his timing is no less than perfect.* Thank you for finding in our favor, we will now be receiving a monthly check and we will be getting backpay. That will help tremendously. Now, my husband will not feel as though he must work a second job. I cannot thank you enough for your blessings on us, God. You are our provider.

GOD'S TOUCH NEEDED AGAIN MANY WAYS

June 5, 1996

Rodney and the boys had two benefit singings this day. One was for a young minister here local. The one at night for a friend of ours, a young lady who has been very ill. She needs assistance with medical bills. They are always ready to help anyone with a need. We have been there and know what it feels like. We also know how it makes you feel to have loving people be willing to come help you in any way they can.

I should be very rested up. I think I have slept just about all week, including today. Even at that, I had to go out to the car and lay down to rest a little while. I could not hold my body up any longer. I was just exhausted. I felt like I must rest for a few minutes, after that, I went back in the church.

I was sitting there meditating and praying about my physical condition and how hard it is to continually fight to stay up and be with my family going anywhere they are scheduled. God began to speak to me, not in an audible voice, but just a revealing one. It seemed he was saying these things to me when I was questioning him as to where he was in all this before. "Do you not know you are walking in the valley of the shadow of death? In the 23rd Psalm it says, "Yea though I walk through the valley of the shadow of death, I will fear no evil for thou art with me..." *Do you not realize that I am the one that has taken all the fear from you concerning your illness. I will be with you to the end of your dilemma to comfort and strengthen you both spiritually and emotionally. I Am the Great I Am.*

The guys have had several concerts lately. One was my favorite church of all times. It was a quaint little church in a quaint little mountain town called Carden Bottoms. I guess I should say it is a little town at the foot of Petit Jean Mountain on the North side. It had an empty parsonage for us to use for the two nights furnished with beds and a kitchen. A very nice place room for all of us. The church and parsonage as well as the surrounding fields reminded me of going to south Arkansas to visit my Grandparents and uncles when I was a kid. Man did it bring back memories, nice nostalgic memories. It was even surrounded by corn fields, and long sandy lanes to take walks on. Just a beautiful countryside home place. I think we all enjoyed that weekend. It was a nice, different weekend getaway. The church members were very sweet, and services were great.

We came home and got right back into the same routine. Everyone went back to work as usual. Me, I rested a day or so, then I had to take care of some business in town. I got on the freeway, set my cruise at between 60-65. Suddenly my car jumped, cruise went off, I have no idea why either of those things happened. When they did, I came to myself, and realized I was just about to run into the truck ahead of me. I do not know how or when I had gotten behind that truck. I just know I was very thankful for whatever it was that woke me up. I don't know if I passed out temporarily or fell asleep or exactly what happened. I only knew that was going to be the end of my driving for a while. I was passing out, falling, legs too weak, as well as too many other things happening. When my husband arrived home, I told him what had happened. My first thought was how God had to be watching over me that day. I have been reading too many Angel books. I had been reading a lot of them and other Christian books about the power of God watching over us. Due to the events of that day, I took myself off driving as of this date, June 28, 1996, until I felt it was safe for me as well as everyone else on the highway again. I had already quit driving a while back with the grandbabies in the car with me. I will only drive if it is necessary from now on and as little as possible and never when I am feeling bad and disoriented. I am not being too particular, just safe for everyone.

Lately I am having some very severe nerve pain, stinging, burning, and feeling like pins sticking in my feet, legs and heels so bad I cry. I can't help myself. My legs just shake, and I can't put my feet on the floor. I almost scream. I try to brush my teeth at the sink in the bathroom holding one foot up at a time, but they hurt so bad, I am about to scream any time. I switch feet and they hurt the same. The pain was getting almost too great to bear.

On Wednesday, July 24, when I saw Dr. Hollis, He discovered my white blood cells were at 11,000, which were indicative of an infection somewhere in my body. My sed rate was at 49, which meant my inflammation was high. No wonder the pain was so severe all over. He prescribed more antibiotics and steroids to help control this to keep it from getting any worse and hopefully get rid of it all. I was feeling a little better by the weekend, but not enough to be going anywhere. I did do my best to be with my family in what they had to do part of the time. My son, and his wife, Damon and Keela, took us out for lunch on Saturday. It was nice to visit with them. They had just moved out of town to their new home. It was nice to visit with them. Sunday Night the guys had a singing a little way from home. Then Monday night they sang on the Riverboat. It is a Gospel Night on a Riverboat on the Arkansas River. They loved being the entertainment on their night. It is a very rewarding and fulfilling night for them. I am proud of and for them. They meet a lot of wonderful new Godly people they have a lot in common with. This time, my daughter-in-law and I went with them. We enjoyed it as well.

I had a very nice surprise on my birthday August 11,1996. My family gave me a surprise birthday party after church. We had an all-church meeting Rodney wanted me to attend, then I was going to go home. I was in a lot of pain and needed to go. He sent the pastor's wife to talk me into staying until church was over. As soon as it was over, they needed me in the fellowship hall. I went and they were waiting for me. I never expected that at all. It was very nice. I received a lot of nice gifts, and I enjoyed the fellowship with everyone. That was very sweet of my family and friends to do that for me.

About a week later August 16, 1996, I had to get another appointment with Dr. Hollis. I was getting sicker by the day and must find out what was going on. I then discovered the reason for feeling so bad and all the pain. My body was full of infection and bacteria. My blood and kidneys had the same bad bacteria in it as before, which will probably prove to be E-Coli. He put me right into the hospital. I was started on IV antibiotics, Tagamet HB Acid Reducer, steroids (Solu-Medrol) or (Methylprednisolone), and pain shots. On the 23rd of August, I had an EGD (light down my throat) to see why I was still so sick at my stomach all time. He said I had Gastritis in my stomach and a fungal infection in my esophagus. Either one or both could contribute to the throwing up. They were both bad enough to cause any thing. The doctor told me today the fungal infection in my esophagus looked like ground hamburger inside. He also said the reason for all these problems is a breakdown in my immune system. I guess that means, my immune system will have to get built back up somehow (whatever that will take) before I will see any improvement and quit practically living in the hospital. I thought I had been doing better until after I ate dinner tonight and I was too weak and in too much pain to go to the restroom. The doctor started trying me on a new kind of pain medication. I prayed it would help better than what I have been taking. I will surely get to go home soon.

At least I am on my favorite floor here. I really love all these nurses here on the fifth floor. We have a wonderful relationship and comradery with each other. They are the best. I have grown to love these ladies, not just as my nurses, but as my friends and family. They are all very special to me.

I think for the first time today, it hit me as to actually where this disease could lead to. I really think it will go into remission, but I know it is possible that it won't and will continue to break down my immune system until I have virtually none. I guess all I can say Is "what will be, will be." I just know that Jesus will be there for me all the way to the end, whatever the end will be. I just hate that my family will go through it with me, and I am putting my husband and them through so much. I wish there was some way I could get around that part of it and go through it by myself. Rodney and I talked a little about it at times and the possibilities. We are not going to dwell on that but make the most of it day by day looking to the future. We also have our affairs in order in planning for the future.

I finally got to go home from the hospital on August 26. I was certainly ready to get out of there. Of course, once again I went home with my supply of medicine and all my things to do and not to do. I was also told I had to think about the fact that I was going to have to have a blood transfusion. That was something I did not want to even think about. It isn't as bad as it used to be, but I still am a bit apprehensive about getting blood because of all the diseases transferred through blood. I will have to pray about that one. I will also have to talk to my doctor about that further when I see him again.

When I got home, I couldn't do anything but bedrest for a few days. I was completely drained. I just rested for a few days and then I gradually was able to be up a little at a time. The last part of the week, I rode over to Hot Springs with Rose to pick up Kevin's check. The boys were so quiet and took in the scenery. They enjoyed the ride. We then stopped and ate a bit of lunch. It was nice to get out, tiring, but nice and enjoyable.

CHAPTER THIRTEEN

MANY THINGS HAPPENING

It is now September 29th, one day before my son and daughter-in-law's anniversary. We are all getting anxious for their new arrival. She is due soon. I have got to get busy to finish her blanket before her shower on the 8th of October. I am crocheting a purple blanket for her. I have been gone from home so much, I am behind in getting it completed. I wish I could stay well for a while and get some things done.

Talking about staying well, I went to church Sunday morning and knew I should not have. I felt so bad, I should have stayed in bed. I was sitting there, began to feel even worse and passed out. Sitting right there on the seat, I went out. I scared two of the older ladies. Not to mention how bad it embarrassed me. I sure hope if that ever happens again, I can make it outside first before going out. I ended up going home, going to bed, and staying for a few days. I had just overexerted my body and exhausted all the energy I had. I had nothing left to go on and could not hold up any longer. Like I said, *God's grace is sufficient. He has a way of stopping you when you have gone as far as your body can take.*

October 19, 1996

> *It doesn't seem possible, but it has been one year since the birth of our first grandchildren, our twin grandsons. Their first birthday party is tonight. It was a wonderful time. I think their mom and dad had more fun opening their presents than they did. LOL. They weren't too interested in the presents. They were more interested in the grandparents. That was fine with us all. We sort of loved that part too. That was an interesting night.*

> *Bless her heart, Missy was miserable tonight. She had a good time with her nephews, but she was definitely ready to have that little girl any time now.*

> *Raymond and Missy's wish was granted not too long after we all got home from the party. Sometime in the early morning hours the next morning, Missy went into labor. She was there a few hours before she was born at 11:01am. Our little beautiful Aleigha was here. We were all so very excited. Our first girl in our family. The doctors said she was a perfectly, healthy little girl.*

It is now November 15, 1996, and our remodeling is finished. We haven't needed to have Raymond and Missy bring the new baby over until we were finished with it. This was our first visit from our new granddaughter.

It was so much fun playing with her and loving on her. She is so beautiful.

I am so looking forward to all my grandchildren getting together and playing together. I am anxious to see them interacting with each other and being best friends. I am going to do my best to get them together as much as possible.

This was a good time to visit. My health is doing better.

I had a very nice luncheon with a very dear friend. We have been special friends for many years. We always have a very special time when we find time to get together. In the last few years, when she has had a chance or time when not working, I haven't been able to go. Therefore, we have been unable to get together. Thank you for giving us time together. We always have a good time talking about how wonderful you are. We always love discussing your Grace and encouragement to us.

Thank you, Lord for giving us what we have need of and the touch we need just in time to keep our faith strong and alive. Thank you also, for bringing to our memory the scriptures we need at the right time. At times you bring scriptures to my mind I need that I didn't even know I knew, and I am so grateful for them. I must ask myself at times, "Where did that one come from?"

"I will lift up mine eyes unto the hills, from whence cometh my help. My help cometh from the lord, which made heaven and earth" (Psalm 121: 1& 2 KJV).

CHAPTER FOURTEEN

LOSING MOM AND LUPUS WON'T PAUSE

*M*other has been ill for a few days, but we weren't sure exactly sure what her problem was. The Home health nurse sent her to the hospital on December 18, 1996. The following Monday they sent her for test. One was an arteriogram. This showed she had an 80 to 90 % blockage in the Carotid Artery. The following Monday they did surgery. This was on 12/30/96. She came through the surgery okay. She was left with some side effects. There was something drawing her mouth, and she has difficulty talking. We are hoping that will clear up with time and healing. The doctors told us she must have 24/7 continuous skilled nursing care. She has agreed to go into a Nursing Facility near me. She seems to have adjusted to the fact this is the way it must be. I think it has helped that my sister has helped. She and her husband have come home from California. They arrived home the day she went in the hospital. By coming home then, she was there for her surgery. That really helped me a lot. I know that isn't why she came, but I'm sure glad she was there. I hadn't told her and any of the family, my siblings, I don't think, I have been taking Rheometric. That is a form of Chemotherapy. I had been on it since December 4th. Dr. Hollis is trying this in an attempt to send me into remission. Boy, that would be nice. But that remains to be seen. So far, I can't tell a lot of improvement in the pain. I am just about to scream on the inside. I don't dare let go of my emotions where I am at this time. These Nursing Home Patient patients would be scared to death and think I had completely lost my mind, and it would not be far from the truth. I managed the pain just fine as long as it stays in my body and leaves my mind alone, but when it begins pressing on my mind, that is when it gets too much to handle. If you have ever been in pain for a long period of time with no relief, that is the only way you would know exactly what I am talking about. The only way I can deal with that kind of pain is to lay down very still, close my eyes and begin to meditate on all good things. Whether it be scriptures, my family, mostly my grandchildren or any number of the many blessings to meditate on or things and people to pray for. I think about the scripture where Paul and Timotheus at Phillippi were talking to the saints and said:

7. And the peace of God, which passeth all understanding, shall keep your hearts and minds through Christ Jesus.

8. Finally, brethren, whatsoever things are true, whatsoever things are honest, whatsoever things are just, whatsoever things are pure, whatsoever things are lovely, whatsoever things are of

good report; if there be any virtue, and if there be any praise, think on these things. Philippians 4:7-8 KJV

I find this to be the best therapy to get my pain settled down and bearable again. It doesn't get rid of it, but it does help.

I use this a lot of time instead of pain medication. **Although the medication works, I take comfort in knowing this method is not going to get me hooked on any medication and I never have side effects.** I usually only took medication when I was not in a place to lie down and use my own remedy and never if I am going to have to drive.

In spite of all that was happening around us we managed to have a beautiful Christmas with our children and grandbabies. We also got together with some of my siblings and Mother. It was not difficult at all with mother since she was almost next door. We would have loved to bring her to my house, but it was not possible as sick as she was. We took Christmas to her.

Mother is settled and content there more than any place she has been since she had her stroke. I think it might be because it is so close to our house and nowhere else she has stayed before has been that near any of us. She has visited me and has stayed with me to recuperate from surgery at other times, so she is very familiar with these surroundings. That makes her comfortable where she is. She was pleased with the personnel. Everything worked out well there.

As for my condition, my health isn't improving much. I had to be admitted to the hospital on January 30, 1997. They diagnosed me with Viral Pneumonitis and Congestive Heart Failure or Fluid in my lungs. I was not released until February 5. I was released to go home to rest and come back to the office in one week. At that time, the fluid was still there. Dr. Hollis sent me to the Hospital for a Heart Ultrasound and said I was to go for further testing. I must go to a Pulmonologist for the treatment of my lungs. The test at the hospital showed they, my lungs, were only operating at 55 to 69%. He didn't know if that was due to the fluid or damage to them. I was praying it was the fluid in them at the time and when that was cleared up, that would be better. Now I guess my next specialist is to be a pulmonologist. I would be glad to go to any doctor to help me breathe better. He said my lungs have lost 25% ability to breathe properly and the outer edges of them are constricted. This means they do not give, expand and contract as I breathe to let the air go in and out. This disease is called Restricted Lung Disease. He increased my Prednisone for the next three weeks, 30 mg the first week, 20 mg second week, 10 mg third week plus added three inhalants and updrafts three to four times a day. My bad cough continued to persist, and my body was very weak for a long time. At least they had improved quite a bit since I was in the hospital. I have been under the treatment of a pulmonologist since that time. I also must have regular Pulmonary Function Test to stay up to date on the progression of the disease. It has not progressed as fast as it could have, but it is worse sometimes more than others.

On July 12, 1997, I was hospitalized once again. This time with severe stomach pains that had been going on for several weeks. They were getting severe and to the point where I could not stand to touch my abdomen at all hardly. I could not get my colon to act at all, I was locked up completely unless I took strong laxatives constantly. When I got to the hospital, the next morning, they performed a test to check my mobility of my stomach they put some radioactive material (at least I think that was what it was from the best I recall) in scrambled eggs and I was to eat them. They took pictures of my stomach afterwards to see how long it took to digest them. They kept the camera on my abdomen for hours and the eggs never moved. There was no movement at all. I was then diagnosed with Gastroparesis, that is where the gastric system is paralyzed and doesn't work. It is a very painful condition, The doctors were treating it with IV steroids, Reglan, Potassium, oral Propulsid, Plus some other things. They are telling me I will have to be careful the rest of my life. I really think it will eventually turn around. I am praying it will anyway. I did not get out of the hospital until July 30th. I was ready to leave.

I spent a short stay in the hospital in September 26 through October 2, mostly for IV steroids to get my Sed rate down and in control again or to try anyway.

Dr. Hollis had to try sending me to a female Rheumatologist. I might like her better, so he thought. I might do it. I do like female doctors usually. I am sure I will like her. I did like her very much.

I saw her shortly after that. She told me of a doctor that treated patients with Gastropareses. She set me up an appointment with him in October. I had a week of testing there to see if I was a good candidate for a gastric pacemaker. She did that because the pain is getting worse. I went back in a couple of weeks to get the results of the tests. The test concluded that I was a very good candidate. He said very seldom do the test show more than three places where a connective tissue disease is present. There were thirteen places in my stomach. The major problem with that, however, is each one costs thousands. It was thousands for each: the hospital, the pacemaker, and the doctor. It is not FDA Approved, and most insurance companies will not pay for any part of it. For me, that is definitely not going to be a priority. There is no way I have that kind of money in the first place, much less for something that has not been tested and has not been approved by the FDA. He had only performed that surgery a few times to know if it would work and how long if at all. The best part of the whole week was Rodney and I had a weeks get away together, except for the testing times, to enjoy each other with no interruptions.

In 1997, I had been hospitalized a total of 4 times. In 1998, a total of 5 in-patient visits were necessary. These were all for the same thing as before, some pretty severe and some the same.

We received more wonderful news in November of a new grandbaby on the way. Our son, Damon and his wife, Keela are having their first child. We are all very excited about this long-awaited new addition.

In 1999 I was hospitalized five times. I had still been having lots of problems with my gastric system plus other things. During that time my lungs were giving me problems. They were collapsed, diagnosed as atelectasis. I also have been having heart problems, myocarditis, and tachycardia. I have been having a lot of difficulty breathing and when I exert any energy at all of which I have very little of, my heart races with a lot of pain in my chest.

June 1, 1999 delivery day for our fourth grandchild and our second granddaughter had arrived. A perfect, healthy, beautiful little redheaded girl, Avorie. We were all very excited. God is so awesome. We had all waited and longed for this day for a long time, especially for our son and daughter-in-law. I was so grateful I was out of the hospital for the birth of my granddaughter. I was not feeling well at all, but I was there, at least.

I was admitted back in the hospital on June 23, 1999. I was very ill. My sed rate was high and I was unable to breathe plus other problems I had to have very strong steroids and antibiotics for an infection. While in the hospital, on June 29th, I received a call from the nursing home my mother was in. She was very ill, and they were transporting her to the hospital to be arriving in the emergency room any time. I could not meet her. I was too ill and hooked up to all kind of tubes, so I called my son and my husband to meet her there. She had a kidney infection that had already set up sepsis. Her white blood count was 29,000 when she got to the hospital. And her blood sugar was 40. The doctor came to see me the next day in my room. He told me the nursing home had waited too late to call the ambulance and get her help and he did not think he could help her. He was going to do everything he could to pull her out of this, but he was afraid all he would be able to do was keep her as comfortable as possible. He was giving her strong IV antibiotics and treating the pain plus everything else possible. Her kidneys failed shortly after that, and she kept going downhill. Her blood sugar went to 840 and she slipped into a coma.

My doctor let me go to her room a couple of times since she was on the same floor before she went into the coma. I got to talk and visit with her while she was able to carry on a conversation with me. I am glad I had visited her a lot before I went into the hospital. We had seen her the night before. I had told the nurse that night to check her urine. It was too dark. She said she would. I called the next two days to see and first day they said they had, next day the nurse said the report was perfectly clear, no bacteria. They could not have checked it with a reading of 29,000 then. I also called another time and checked on her they said she was fine. I talked my doctor into releasing me on July 3rd so I could be with my mother more before she passed. I told him I would come back if I needed to when it was all over. He was reluctant, but finally agreed to let me go. I was not well, had to use a wheelchair and rest a lot, but I got to stay with her quite a bit and was free to come and go as I was able.

On July 10, 1999, at about 6:30 a.m., Mother woke up out of the coma, looked around, could not talk, she looked toward heaven and pointed. We could see a longing in her eyes.

Raymond and Damon had just sang "Wish You Were Here "and our Pastor was reading what Heaven is like at about 11:30 when Mother just slowly quit breathing with a peaceful look on her face drifted off to a forever sleep into the arms of Jesus. That was a very hard and sad day for all of us, as well as the next few months of missing her. She had always been our mother and father all our life. I was busy for the next few months taking care of her business since she had made me power of attorney of her estate quite a number of years before I became ill. Fortunately, I was able to take care of most of it by phone. It wasn't difficult since she had made the decisions with her attorney. I didn't mind at all, after all, this was the last thing I could have ever done for her.

CHAPTER FIFTEEN

A New Century- 2000 – Better or Not ??

This part of the new century can't get any better. You will never improve on perfection and my grandbabies are as perfect as they can possibly be. They are growing up so beautifully. The twins, Kyle and Cole are now four years old. My first granddaughter, Aleigha, is three years and Avorie, is seven months. My how time flies!

The older three are a lot more knowledgeable of the bible than I realized. I was asking Kyle and Cole some questions about Daniel, Noah, and Adam & Eve, etc. They could answer every one of them. Aleigha can recite almost all the 23rd Psalm by herself. They are all very intelligent to know all that they do and just be 3 and 4 years old plus all the schoolwork they know. They spent the night with me on April 8th. We were all sleeping on the waterbed. I was telling them stories of *The Three Little Pigs*, *The Three Bears*, etc. They wanted to hear Bible stories. When it was time to go to sleep, Cole reminded me we had to say our prayers, he wanted to pray, and we repeated after him. It was the sweetest, most heartwarming prayer ever. The twins had stayed before, but this was the first time Aleigha had stayed. I can't wait until the next time and when Avorie can stay with us.

I started the year off as usual, in the hospital at least some time in January. This year, it was January 20th through January 28th. The next time was March 2-6, followed by April 13-19. The first two times this year were my sed rate and my lungs. My breathing was progressively getting worse. Each time I go to the hospital with my lungs bothering me, they get a little worse. I am not sure exactly what the problem is and why, but I know I feel like I am smothering. The pain in my entire body is getting harder to control. It doesn't work to lay down and meditate to get rid of the pain anymore. The pain is too great.

When I was hospitalized on April 13-19, the test showed my lungs had collapsed again; atelectasis. I was also being treated for neuropathy, vasculitis, and severe pain. I was so miserable. Not to mention I was given oxygen again.

Just a little over a month later, May 30-June 5, I had to go right back in for the same problems. High Sed rate, lot of inflammation, lung problems, breathing difficulties, etc.

Kyle and Cole got to spend the night with me again between these two hospital visits. Aleigha stayed until 10:00. They had to leave the next morning to go out of town for a family get together.

It seemed no matter how hard I tried, I could not seem to get well, can't seem to do anything to help myself and I try so hard to take care of myself. I do what the doctors say to do, take the medication they say, rest when I get tired, keep all my appointments, go to the specialist and all the things that I have to do.

Sometime in the next few hospitalizations in some of my test the doctors had found that I had evidence of a stroke on one side of my brain. Within the next year, they found I had two more. I knew when I had the first two. However, the third one, I am not sure of. The first one, I was unable to read for a week or so. The second, I went blind for a short period of time. Both these times were very scary. The third one was on the base of my brain.

On July 6th the doctor admitted me back in the hospital for several reasons, because my sed rate was outrageously high, out of control diabetes, and Neuropathy was so painfully unbearable. I was put on all the usual medications immediately. I finally got out on the twelfth of July. By then I was feeling much better, but I still had a way to go to be completely well.

AUGUST 9, 2000

Rodney wanted to get away for a few days. He asked me if I thought I was up to just taking a ride around in the state for a few days. I really felt like I could use it too. We got up the next morning and took off. We didn't want to forget our new wheelchair and walker. That will be a lifesaver. Not only that, but there is also no way I could go to anything with my husband without one or the other. We just went to Pine Ridge to the Lum and Abner's Jot-em-down store for a little bit of nostalgia. When we left there, we went up through Mountain View and spent the night there. We went to the Ozark Folk Center the next day. We had a nice trip, and it was nice to get away.

On our way back home, we went to our sons to pick up our granddaughter to spend the night with us. When we got there, the kids were all there to give me a surprise birthday party. Missy had my favorites. It was very sweet of her to do that for me. It was all very delicious, as usual.

I was hospitalized again on August 23-29. The middle of August, my heart began to race again. I had that trouble before, but it seemed to be under control. Of course, I knew it was the lupus, but I wasn't sure what it is doing to my heart. I could just stand to my feet, and it would go up to 130. If I did exert any energy, it would go to 155-170 plus. If I didn't sit down quickly, I would pass out where I stood.

I was in and out of the hospital three more times in the year of 2000 (October 11-16, November 8-10, and December 12-15). My heart continued to race, and my lungs were not opening at all any more than they had been. My sed rate was progressively increasing in number.

By this time in this disease, I was getting so weak it was so hard for me to get around to get anywhere. My husband had to do just about all the shopping. Every once in a while, I would go with him if we only had a very few things to pick up. Then sometimes he would have to take me out to the car before we were finished. Sometimes I think I can't go much further. I knew I couldn't without a new portion of strength from God, I had to start waking up every day, set up on the side of the bed, pray and tell God, *Okay God; this one is yours; I can't do it. I have no strength without you to supply it to even start this day. Please God, go with me through this day, Bless me so I can bless others. Help me complete the task I need to complete for my family. Thank you in Jesus' name.* It wasn't aways easy and I had to rest a lot, use the aid of my walker, etc. most of the time with the aid of God, I completed most of what was important.

The next year brought some very hard times for me. I was in the hospital a lot in the year of 2001. January 31-Feb 2, March 14-16, and March 23-28, my heart was racing really bad as well as other things was going wrong. The doctor was trying to get it to settle down and find a medication that would work on the problem. He tried me on Topral XL 150mg 2 per day and Trazac 300 mg/day. That's the medication I went home with. I was sure praying that was going to work.

I guess the medicine worked for a little while. I didn't go back to the hospital until May 7th. I had all the same things wrong with me. My sed rate was always one of the things he had to treat. It was always up and that was always one of the main things they did not want to be up, not even in the 20's and mine was always far above that. Many times, I did not know how high it was, but my body sure told me it was high. I was released on the 12th of May, 2001.

I was doing pretty good when I got out of the hospital, so I thought. By that afternoon, I began to feel very ill. The next morning, I felt even more ill. I had no idea what was wrong and why I was already getting so sick so quickly after being given all the IV medication that helps so much. All I knew is I was not well at all for some reason. That day was Mother's Day. My son and his wife, Raymond and Missy came over and prepared Mother's Day lunch for us. Although I was very appreciative, I could not get out of bed. I tried with everything in me, and I could not raise my body up. I don't think I had, even at that time had ever been so sick in all my life. I told them, please forgive me, but I could not come in there and I could not eat. I went on like that until May 16th. Then I couldn't even get up with my husband's help to go to the restroom, my eyes wouldn't focus, my legs burned to touch, and I was feeling worse than I had ever felt in my entire life. When my husband came in our bedroom, I told him to call the ambulance. I said I am not going to get any better, I am getting worse by the minute.

They came right away and took me to the hospital. The first thing they did was run blood tests. They said my potassium was at 2, my doctor said my sodium was lower than he had ever seen. He said he did not know how I was still alive. I was completely dehydrated. They had to put an IV in and could not get it, so they had to put a central line in me. My potassium was at 2 and my sodium was lower than my doctor had ever seen before. He didn't know how I was still here. I was totally dehydrated also. I was terribly sick to begin with and too weak to get up. Then somehow, I was infected with staph infection and became even more ill. My temperature went up to 104.6 and maybe higher. That is just the highest I knew of. This was very surprising to me. That was the first time I had ran a temperature since I was diagnosed with Lupus. The doctors told me it was because my body did not fight anything helping me get rid of disease and bacteria. I guess this was a good thing, at least this time my body was fighting for me.

Of all things, the IV had to come out and replace the central line. I was still too dehydrated to get an IV back in so they had to put a central line back in. The doctor that was there that night put it in an artery, not a vein. It was hurting. He left it there and an LPN found it was inserted in the wrong place. He came back. No lidocaine, nothing at all to help me, he took that one out, moved to the other side, again no lidocaine or numbing of any kind. He was moving it around, in and out, in and out. I told them I was very sick in my stomach over and over. He said he would order me something in a minute when he got finished. I told him I was about to throw up. It was hurting so bad it was making me sick. Someone said I had to have it; I was too sick not to get it in. I told them I could not take it anymore. I said if you don't get it now, quit and get someone else. He got it about that time. Just in time, I told the nurse to give me an emesis basin, I was going to throw up, and I thought I wasn't going to quit. I filled up two or three of the basins. I was sick for the longest time that night. I had to stay in the hospital until June 8th.

I was not able to get up and down on my own very well when I went home. The therapist at the hospital ordered me a walker and a lightweight wheelchair to take home with me. An appliance company delivered them to me. I had to take therapy for a while to try to get my legs to work. The doctor ordered home therapy for me. Rodney would have had to take off work to take me to the therapy center two or three times a week or more. He had been taking me on all my doctor appointments since I wasn't able to drive and didn't mind so if there was a way to get around it, I needed to do that. Also, I had no idea how long I would be taking therapy. I took therapy as long as my insurance would let me, and my legs and body were still not strong enough to operate efficiently enough for me to feel comfortable and trustworthy. I continued to exercise on my own with a few small tools the therapist left for me. That was very nice of him to do. It took a long time. I was continually working on this because as soon as I was getting a little stronger, I would get sicker and go downhill. Then I would have to work back up again. At least God did let me get able to work back up to at least where I was. I was still having to use my walker for a while after that. I needed it for stability a little and to keep from falling. I did not want to fall and break my hip or leg. That is something my Neurologist cautions me about ever since I was diagnosed with Neuropathy in my feet and legs. He thinks I need to use a walker or at least a cane all time. I have been told, with Neuropathy, the signals going from your feet to your brain can get confused and make you fall easily. I guess it was very important for me to use them because I was not good at keeping my balance before the neuropathy since the weakness of the Lupus.

All the time I was in the house trying to learn to walk again and getting my stamina back, my husband was on the back working on a large deck, 26'X12'. He put in lot of hours building it for me and did a great job.

I also must remember to have my central line flushed at the hospital every thirty days if it is not used. That is very important to keep it flowing freely and not clogged up.

Dr. Hollis had decided to send me to a cardiologist that specializes in abnormal heart rhythms. I had several appointments with him in the later part of 2001. First, he put me through a series of test. One was a Tilt table test. That one made me sick at my stomach. Another test, for another day that also made me quite ill, was a nuclear Stress Test. I have never understood why they want to stress your heart out to the point of being so ill. It makes no sense at all to me. I don't remember what all he ordered. They were all in the office except the Tilt table and it was at a hospital. Of course, my husband was always right there with me when I got so very sick with all the things they were doing to me. Thank God because I would not have been able to drive home after some of them. I will say to those reading this: I know these tests do not affect everyone the way they do me. I have a very weak gastric system. My lungs and my heart are not very strong either so with all that together, I can't take much at all. Just about everything makes me sick.

There were two more admissions to the hospital, August 28th through September 4th, and November 5th through 9th, and two outpatient procedures, Sept 26th and Sept 27th.

On November 13th, my third granddaughter and fifth grandchild was born, Emery. She looked like a beautiful little redheaded doll. Like with the twins, my son and his wife got it approved for me to be in the room when she was born. This was a very special privilege to me. I am so very grateful to her parents for such an honor. I will always remember. Thank you so very much!

CHAPTER SIXTEEN

MORE HEART PROBLEMS – ABLATION

*A*fter I began going to the cardiology specialist, and all the tests were over and back, the doctor, Dr. Ballard, who was treating me wanted us to come back in to discuss how he would like to treat this problem. The next day at my appointment, we went into his office, he proceeded to explain what he was planning on doing.

He said the procedure was called an Ablation. It is used to treat Atrial fibrillation; it uses small burns or freezes to cause some scaring on the inside of the heart to help break up the electrical signals that cause irregular heartbeats. This can help the heart maintain a normal heart rhythm. He set up the procedure for January 14, 2002. I am to go to my PCP, Dr. Hollis the day before checking in at the hospital to make sure I was up to the procedure otherwise.

I did as he asked me to, and my sed rate was quite high and a few other things needed to be treated. Dr. Hollis and Dr. Ballard agreed for me to go from the hospital that Dr. Ballard was at to the one Dr. Hollis was at the next morning and check in there. I would be treated by Dr. Hollis as usual and recuperated from the ablation at the same time. I didn't have any problem from the ablation except my chest burned inside sometimes. I could tell something had been done in there. It all went pretty well. I was released from the hospital on the 21st of January.

My heart seamed to settle down almost immediately. It was beating at a regular rhythm. I could breathe a little better also. I had no idea how bad my heartbeat was and how it was affecting my whole existence until I was feeling better. I owed them a big thank you. I will take care of that for sure.

Even though I still had all the other problems popping up causing hospitalization, March 11-15 and May 6-13, I wasn't having a racing heart, thank God. That was a blessing.

On July 7, 2002, we had a wonderful, but a bit scary surprise. We were blessed with our fourth granddaughter, Josie. A gorgeous, little dark headed bundle of joy. She was 5 weeks early. She and mother are perfectly fine. God is Good!

The next day, I was admitted right back in the hospital. Plus, three more times before the end of the year; July 8-13, September 30-October 4, November 18-November 22, and December 18-31. There were the same problems all the time over and over. I won't go into those again and again, the same routines every time I am hospitalized. You would become bored even more than you already are.

The bad part about all this sickness was some of my grandkids had started school and were playing sports. That means they were having concerts, shows, skits, ball games, etc. I had been missing so much. I knew I had missed soccer games and some choir concerts, and I had no idea what else. The twins had asked me why I didn't come to their soccer game. Sometimes, I had been in the hospital and sometimes, I was just not able. They acted like they understood. It sure hurts my heart to know they wish I was there, and I could not be for them. It is such a joy to watch them all learning so much, so quickly. I can't help but get mad at this disease for taking time away from my grandchildren and me. On the same level, I must thank God for giving me the privilege to be with them despite the disease as much as I have. His grace has been very sufficient for all I have had need of. They still spend the night with us or me a lot between hospitalizations. Sometimes grandpa sleeps through it because he is so tired from working.

In 2003, I was admitted to the hospital a total of eight times. They were for the same problems I have been treated for prior. Most of them were due to my sed rate being so high, and other things.

Also, we had another grandson born on May 23 of 2003. He was given the name of Ethan. Again, his parents, Damon and Keela allowed me to be in the room when he was born. We were blessed to have another healthy, handsome baby boy.

Once again, God gave a warning: In December of this same year Rodney kept feeling like he needed to have a colonoscopy and a physical. We made an appointment with our primary care physician, Dr. Hollis. His physical went ok, and he set up the colonoscopy. When he came out of the procedure, Dr. Silas said, "Rodney, Sir wake up, we need to talk." That startled me a little. He said he had removed a lot of polyps, about twelve or so. However, there were three he was unable to remove with the scope. They were so large; they were categorized as an abdominal mass times two. They must be removed surgically.

The new year had arrived, and my utmost thought was to get my husband through this surgery. God was going to give me strength to help him through whatever he was facing, and we were going to get through it together.

Rodney's surgery was scheduled for January 8, 2004. The surgery ended up being quite extensive. The surgeon, Dr. Willis had to remove sixty percent of his colon. He made a wonderful recovery. The test was noncancerous, but there were precancer cells. He was instructed to repeat the procedure every six months to a year which he did. Everyone he had, there were several more polyps to be removed just as before, precancerous cells. We had to keep this checked like he said every six months to a year no matter what else was going on around us. My husband was not an easy person to talk into doing what he was supposed to do medically, so I knew I had to make the appointment for him, then tell him. I was prepared to do just that as I had done so many times before. I made his appointment every six to nine months as soon as they had an opening.

For some reason my immune system was dropping even lower than ever. The doctors have told me not to go to hospitals except as the patient and not go to closed, crowded places. Church was the worse place to go, they said, because people tend to have very close contact. I am taking chances in catching anything. It was best to just stay home, he said.

I was admitted to the hospital five times and several outpatient procedures in the year of 2004 and five inpatient admissions. I was admitted to the hospital in the year 7 times in 2005 and had several outpatient procedures.

By this time, Emery and Josie had become quite the little singers. They had beautiful voices and they each knew all of several songs. I loved for them to sing to me. Those two, along with Avorie and Ethan, were added to my grandma sleepovers.

A lot of these outpatient visits were to flush out my port, in the years after I was discharged on June 8, 2001. I always had to have that taken care of if not admitted back in the hospital 30 days after discharged. Some could have been for IVP's, Colonoscopy, my port flushed or maybe a mammogram or two. Between those, being in and out of the hospital whether inpatient or outpatient, I was usually reading Christian literature, the bible, watching movies, as well as anything to keep my heart and mind uplifted. I wanted to always keep upbeat and not let all the problems brought on by this disease make me unhappy and hard to get along with when my husband came home from work. We were always very happy in our marriage, and we weren't going to allow this to come between us.

While watching television during those years, I managed to crochet everyone in my family large Afghan's and all the grand-children bedspreads, plus all the babies' blankets and some sweater sets.

In the year 2006 and 2007, I was admitted as an inpatient twelve times and several times for outpatient procedures. Plus, in the middle of all the inpatient and outpatient trips to the hospital, my husband had a lot of things going on; several surgeries. To have the surgeries, of course, you must have previous doctor visits. We always tried to support each other in those things. I went to almost all the office visits with him, and all the hospital visits, even though I knew I wasn't supposed to. I felt like I had to, this was my husband. That was where I belonged, right by his side.

On June 22, 2006, I had a right heart cath. It went well and I recuperated nicely.

Four days later Rodney had surgery: Prostate cancer. He had blood tests at the Primary Care Physician's. The doctor sent him to the urologist for further tests. They showed cancer. He had the surgery on June 26, 2006, by robotic means. They were able to remove all the cancer. He was back at work in just a few weeks.

In about the last of September in the year of 2006, we found out we were expecting our eighth grandchild.

On about January 24th, our daughter-in-law, KJ, went for her checkup. Her doctor found there was something going wrong with the placenta. She sent her straight to the hospital to the nearest neonatal ICU, the University Hospital. She was to be put on complete bed rest and on 24-hour monitors until the baby was born. This beautiful, blond headed, blue eyed baby boy was born January 31, 2007, a 26 week gestation baby at a weight of one pound two and one half ounces, named Gabriel. He was kept in Neonatal Intensive Care Unit until his due date, May 3, 2007. He was what we called our Miracle baby. We were told he was going to have a lot done to him. The truth is nothing was wrong. It was so amazing. God is an awesome God. Mother and baby were just fine. She was so amazing as well. After just having surgery to give him life, you couldn't keep her down. She was there to see her son every day. She was so proud of her little miracle. He is a very handsome young man now. This grandson of ours was amazing. He was not slow to learn at all like you would think he would be. He was very quick to learn, talking before he was hardly one. He was trying to move a gate one day that his parents put up to block the doorway when he was just a little over one, little bitty, short baby. He said, "Help, I'm stuck." I was shocked! I had no idea he could talk like that. I asked my son, "Did you hear him?" He said "Sure, he talks like that all time."

The first part of 2007, I was transferred to a new Rheumatologist, Dr. Howard, a very nice doctor. He discovered I was anemic in a lot of vitamins, some are B-12, Vitamin D, Iron, Calcium, and others. He said my immune system was so low and my B12 and Vitamin D were low enough that I was in danger of getting Alzheimer's. He started me on all kinds of vitamins and other medicines' too. He also diagnosed me with Pulmonary Hypertension. He made a list of 29 diagnoses proven with exams and test. Except for being extremely tired, I seemed to be feeling a little better already.

One other thing that took place in 2007 was on August 5, 2007. My husband had surgery again. This time it was for a hernia repair in his abdomen. Everything went well with the surgery and the recovery. I am thankful for God's faithfulness to extend grace to Rodney and me through his surgeries the last few years.

The next year, 2008, I went for 6 inpatient hospital visits and several (at least 6) outpatient visits to the hospital I am pretty sure and possibly more. I am sure at least six of them would have been to flush my port. It was getting hard to take some time. I think my port is getting old and hard to use, maybe a bit over used. It was beginning to give me trouble; it was burning and hurting.

I am feeling better, except for the port giving me problems. I think I can start getting off the prednisone now. My next visit to him, I started going down on it, with a chart from him, I was off it in a few months. The weight started coming off immediately in no time, I was back to me. I still don't know how and why I began to start feeling better. I just did. Dr. Howard told me not to ever take steroids again.

I needed the port out. On 3/16/09 I went to Dr. Davis who put it in. It had a red ring around it. He drew a line around it so he could keep a chart of how fast the infection was growing. He would not take it out. I passed out while he was examining me and mashing around on it where it was infected. My husband and I both told him to take it out before it makes me any sicker. He still would not. He prescribed antibiotics and had me come back in a few days.

3/19/09 It was still swollen and infected. The infected area was larger now, they would not take it out yet.

3/24/09 Doctor's appointment with Dr. Davis at the hospital, Saturday. Infected/red area much larger than red line around port he drew. Still would not take it out.

3/27/09 Dr. taking Dr. Davis's place at office; infection was growing.

3/30/09 Dr. Davis; Infection was getting worse he believed it would get better with these antibiotics, even though I kept getting more ill. I told him I wanted it out and Rodney confirmed it also with each visit.

4/2/09 Dr. Davis; Same thing

4/13/09 Port flushed

4/17/09 Dr Carmichael (new PCP) Admitted to hospital. A hospital cardiologist performed a test and ran a light down my throat and looked in my heart for infection. Test showed bacteria in my blood and heart valves.

4/20/09 My next step was to get started in getting that port out. On the 20th, the port came out.

I still had to have IV antibiotics for six more weeks. Once I was well enough to go home, I had to give them to myself again at home.

When they took the port out, I bled out all in my chest cavity. A year later, I had a mammogram, and found what they said was a mass, but couldn't figure it out. I remembered the blood in my chest and told them. They didn't know if that could be it or not. After a few more mammograms I finally quit going. I had one more mammogram; it was fine.

That was the last time I was hospitalized for Lupus. I have been hospitalized several times since then for similar things, but not on the same caliber. I still have all the same problems, but God has touched my body. I can live a halfway normal life, one not without pain, doctors' visits, medications to help the damage Lupus has caused. I have to watch my limitations and stop when reached. I am far from being in remission. Without God healing me, I will always have lupus. It is not curable. I will always suffer with it in one way or another, but as I said, "God's Grace Is Sufficient" for whatever we need.

"Pay attention, Look Around,"

"Watch God Work" Then "Look Up".

CHAPTER SEVENTEEN

BACK OUT IN THE WORLD

hen we are going through life's ups and downs of our own, if we will look around, we will see there are others just as bad or worse than we are. When I was growing up, my mom always taught us to share whatever we had. If we saw a need and we had any amount at all of what was needed, we were to share, no matter what it was. She said, "There is always more where that came from." We knew she usually meant from God in some way. He was going to meet our need. It was always better to give than to receive. I was told that a lot.

"But my God will supply all your need according to His riches in glory by Christ Jesus" (Phil. 4:19 KJV).

God has it all, He has all supplies, including healing for diseases, atonement for your sins, food for your soul, food for your body. He is the God of plenty. Isn't it wonderful to know God will never run out of anything we have need of?

It is also a wonderful feeling when you see someone in need to stop and help them, or maybe buy their groceries, pay their utilities, rent, or whatever it is they are lacking to get them by. Maybe it is a dish you need to make for them. I am very blessed. I have had family and friends while sick to help me make sure meals are available. However, there are a lot of people that is not the case for. I find, even while sick, it makes me feel better to do things for others like that. I have to use more energy and sometimes it might make me sick for a little while, but it gets my mind off me and my problems. It lets me think about someone else for a while. It is very good therapy. I feel like I have accomplished something worthwhile. I have been known to, when I wasn't able to bake or cook, I would get my husband to take me through a drive through and pick up something for someone.

It doesn't have to be anything that is going to cost you anything. Sometimes, it can be whatever you have that you have no more need of, that can be a treasure to others.

I was going through a closet a few years ago, for instance, and found some totes of blankets and bedspreads used for my son's beds when they were at home. They were in really nice condition. I washed and freshened them up and called the chaplain of the local Police, Fire, Coroner, etc. Departments and asked her if she would have need of them. She was pleased to get them. There had been a house fire where there were several children involved and they needed them. I was so glad to give them to someone who had such a special need. You never know who might need things like that.

I just wanted to let you know, even though you are not able to do a lot of things, there are things you can do to help people. Everything you do for someone else, will make you feel a little better about yourself and how you are still able to do some things. You are proving to yourself you are still okay for some things. There is still something you can do and there is still a chance you can get back out there in the real world someday. Look at me, I was out for a very long time, from1994 to 2009. In 2010, I started really getting out by myself, doing my job as a housewife and mother, and driving again in 2009. I am not well by any means. I am not in remission; I'm still on medication for the disease and the damage it has caused, but totally off all pain medication or narcotics of any kind. I refused to take it several years ago because of my age. I use meditation to deal with the pain. Not even over the counter pain relievers. I am allergic to a lot of them. Not that I am not in a lot of pain, but I choose other means. Lupus patients aren't supposed to take over the counter medication at all unless approved by your physicians. There is too much danger in damaging your internal organs, especially your kidneys and liver. Be very careful of that.

Don't give up. God is not finished with you yet. Keep fighting, keep holding to His hand and don't let go. He is there for you. I know everyone's case is different, and the outcome is not the same. I have heard this a lot lately and I know it to be true, WHAT HE DOESN'T KEEP YOU FROM, HE WILL KEEP YOU THROUGH! I know this because since I have come through all this, I have gone through the hardest and worst obstacle and heartache I ever thought I would have to face. I did not think I would get through this one. God has carried me through it where there has only been one set of footprints in the sand almost all the way. I have made it so far only with His help. I am still struggling with this one and probably will until God calls me home to be with Him and the one I lost. I have learned to be content here, but not satisfied here without the love of my life with me. *I try to keep my mind filled with things above as He instructed us to do. But this road I am traveling now is a much more difficult one than I ever thought possible. I know God is faithful for this one too. I have not only learned to be content, but, I have learned one more very important truth: "When God is all you have, He is all you ever needed in the first place. Look to Him. Lean on Him. Believe His Promises. His word is true."*

One of my goals when I began writing this book was to show others, no matter how sick or in pain you are, you can have a good life with your family. As I began reminiscing those years, I also began studying scriptures, and watching biblical videos to help me. I realized God was encouraging me to complete this project for myself as much as anyone. I pray it encourages many others, but for now I am thanking God for the blessings I have felt and the lessons I have learned in working on this project He has so very graciously helped me complete.

God, please help me to keep this scripture in my mind and in my Heart and never let go of it. This is my desire.

Let the words of my mouth, and the meditation of my heart be acceptable in thy sight, O LORD, my strength, and my redeemer. Psalm 19:14 KJV

ABOUT THE AUTHOR

M. Rosette Cleghorn was born in Fordyce Arkansas and was raised in Sheridan, Arkansas. She married Rodney Cleghorn and they have 3 sons. Rosette worked in the field of Accounting prior to receiving the Lupus diagnosis. She was working in Full Charge Bookkeeping at the time of the diagnosis. In her spare time, she likes to crochet and make quilts. Rosette loves bible study and though she has several favorite bible verses, among her two favorite are the the following:

"And the King shall answer and say unto them, Verily I say unto you, Inasmuch as ye have done it unto one of the least of these my brethren, ye have done it unto me." Matthew 25:45 KJV

"And I have put my words in thy mouth, and I have covered thee in the shadow of mine hand, that I may plant the heavens, and lay the foundations of the earth, and say unto Zion, Thou art my people." Isaiah 51:16

J. Kenkade
School *of Publishing*

**Do you have a story to tell?
Need help writing it?**

Courses held on Saturdays in person
and Wednesdays via Zoom

Interested?
Call (501) 482-1000 or Email us at
info@jkenkadepublishing.com

Also Available from this Author

ISBN: 978-1-944486-48-8
Visit www.amazon.com
Author: Margaret Joanne Rice

Set in the Old South after the Civil War– specifically on a tobacco plantation in Staunton, Virginia– this story revolves around three key groups of people. Plantation owners, plantation workers, and Native Americans play integral roles in this saga. They often intersect and prove necessary for each other to exist in their sociopolitical climate. The conflict in the story involves an ancient Indian folktale about a baby skull hidden on plantation property in a grandfather clock that is shrouded in superstition. This skull is said to have magical powers, and when it disappears, many strange events begin to unfold.

Also Available from
J. Kenkade Publishing

ISBN: 978-1-944486-55-0
Visit www.amazon.com
Author: Garrett Cottrell

In this dystopian novel, a group of teens with superhuman strength find out through a group of Hunters that they must either go on the run to survive or be forced to go to camps set aside for "Abnormals." They decide to go on the run and train in their newly found powers. They gain friends and lose friends along the way, but they fight well together.

Also Available from
J. Kenkade Publishing

ISBN: 978-1-944486-88-7
Visit www.amazon.com
Author: Marshall B Crowder and Luz Eneida Torres

The Wanderer's Enduring Love is a love story that spans centuries. Beginning in the 18th century with Lusamba and Marcelo. A young couple full of life and love that get torn apart by the brutal transatlantic slave trade. In a second attempt at love, Lusamba tries again with Elias, only to be horrifically denied. Modern day couple Neida and Marcel meet on a dating site and immediately realize that they have too much in common for their meeting to be merely coincidental. They decide to explore any connections they might have through DNA testing and soon discover that they have a shared past. Are they prepared for what they might discover? How are they connected? Will what they find bring them closer or tear them apart? Follow them and travel to Cameroon, Puerto Rico, California, Georgia, and Arkansas. See how they use modern technology to uncover the past and discover their future.

Also Available from J. Kenkade Publishing

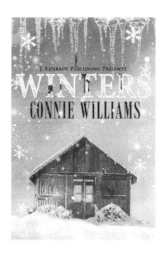

ISBN: 978-1-944486-40-2
Visit www.amazon.com
Author: Connie Williams

Winters is a captivating and passionate Christian suspense novel about a powerful, spiritual black family who is anointed and ordained by God Almighty. You will feel love, pain, heartaches, compassion, grace, mercy, suffering, and God's spirit, all in one story. Find out why Winters is about the coldest season of the year in more ways than one. Come and live in the minds and hearts of Stella, Abe, Mr. Perkins, The Langley family, Hattie, Benjamin, and Minnie. So much more awaits you in this powerful Christian suspense novel. Both fiction and nonfiction, Winters will give you a chill like never before!

Made in the USA
Columbia, SC
23 February 2025

0b58353a-bd0a-468e-8bf0-398d28e86e47R02